Effective Supply Teaching

Effective Supply Teaching

Behaviour Management, Classroom Discipline and Colleague Support

Bill Rogers

P·C·P
Paul Chapman
Publishing

First published 2003

Paul Chapman Publishing
A SAGE Publications Company
6 Bonhill Street
London EC2A 4PU

SAGE Publications Inc
2455 Teller Road
Thousand Oaks, California 91320

SAGE Publications India Pvt Ltd
B-42, Panchsheel Enclave
Post Box 4109
New Delhi 100 017

Library of Congress Control Number 2002 113049

A catalogue record for this book is available from the British Library

ISBN 0 7619 4227 0
ISBN 0 7619 4228 9 (pbk)

Typeset by Anneset, Weston-super-Mare, Somerset
Printed and bound in Great Britain by Athenaum Press, Gateshead

Acknowledgements

To all my colleagues who teach as supply teachers, who have allowed me to work with them in their classrooms and in workshops over the years.

My thanks to all the team at Paul Chapman Publishing who have supported this project from the outset. My special thanks to the editorial team, particularly Marianne Lagrange, Saleha Nessa and Jeanette Graham.

Bill Rogers
August 2002

Contents

The English novelist George Eliot said 'What do we live for if it is not to make life less difficult for each other?' At the heart of colleague support is that shared humanity, without which any meaningful common activity is much more difficult. The days are long gone when teachers had to work in professional isolation, anxious perhaps that others might negatively assess and rate them. Collaboration and collegiality are not simplistic notions or some easy formula for 'successful support'; rather they are the necessary condition for likely, constructive and purposeful support in our profession. When colleagues believe and feel they are valued, both their basic human needs as well as their professional needs are more likely to be met. I hope this book will support that aim.

1

Introduction: the natural challenges of supply teaching

O, how full of briers is this working-day world!
(Shakespeare, *'As You Like It' I: iii*)

You're not our normal teacher!
(*Every tenth student to a supply teacher*)

I began teaching many years ago as an ET (an emergency teacher as we were then called in the 1970s). The current term in Victoria (Australia) is CRT – casual relief teacher, equivalent to a 'supply teacher'. The term 'supply' conjures up for me a teacher bringing relief supplies to 'the beleaguered garrison . . . '.

My first day as an ET is well remembered. I drove into the car park of the school, a rather shabby looking primary school with many students already at play, by 8.15 a.m. As I headed for the office several 'lads' came over and noisily started hassling me, 'Ay; you gonna be our teacher?!' 'What's your name?' 'Why you here?' 'You gonna take Ms Snaggs's class . . . ?' ('I hope not,' I thought.)

As I walked to the front office I saw a mother yelling at another adult – who I assumed was a teacher – 'Yeah well you never cared for our Jayson did yuh! You never gave him a break! This is a sh-t school . . . !' I walked past hoping her Jayson wasn't in my class that day. The principal (head teacher) looked really frazzled already; he was glad to see me. 'Are you the ET? Sorry. What's your name?' We chatted all too briefly. 'Yes.' 'You've got 6F. All the best. Room 17. See Richard or Judy, OK – staff room.' He had that short-sentence way of speaking, like morse code. He hurried off in the direction of Jayson's mum who could still be heard even inside the building 'Sorry. Got to go.' 6F were noisy, brash, challenging, fractious and attentional – and that was in the corridor 'lining' up! It seemed to takes ages for them to settle down, but we eventually got going and actually got some work done. There were students who were brought some unusual and provocative toys to class that day; students who were skilled at task-avoiding, who called out repeatedly; students who seemed to think that classroom conversations could be conducted at playground noise level. Several students came late to class that morning, had forgotten or mislaid pens and personal equipment (I quickly wondered how much of that was intentional). Calling out, butting in and talking while I was trying to gain whole-class attention was a repeated challenge throughout the day but mostly in the first 15–20 minutes. One student jumped out of the window and 'did a runner', just before morning recess (ground floor thankfully!).

I asked myself many questions that day; some quickly, some at the day's end:

- What sort of discipline language should I use? What is a better way of making my leadership firm, clear, without looking 'bossy', 'mean' or 'weak'?
- Should I confiscate toys – how?
- What do I do/say when students are late? Do I notify the office?
- The boy who 'did a runner' – how could I deal with that kind of incident more effectively next time?

I was a mature-age 'beginning' teacher and that helped a little (at least I didn't *look* like a neophyte).

I had many students ask me, as a matter of course, when I was going to become a 'real teacher'. They had in their minds a comparative conception between 'regular' and 'occasional' teacher; as 'real' is to 'non-real'. I taught in many, many schools like this one over the early years as a supply teacher before I became a 'real' teacher. What I learned as a supply teacher became my proving ground as a so-called 'full-time' teacher.

Many of the skills, and approaches, I eventually learned I have outlined in this book. Experience can be a helpful teacher but *experience* of itself does not tell you what to do in the sorts of situations typically faced by supply teachers. This book does not so much tell you 'what' to do, but it does share the issues faced by all supply teachers and outlines particular approaches – even *specific skills of discipline* – that my colleagues and I have found helpful and supportive.

A typical day?

You arrive early, you go to the front office to find out which class you have. You received a phone call last night (or even at 8.00 a.m. that morning!).

You look through the little glass sliding door under the sign that says 'Office'. The school secretary looks distracted – very distracted. 'Yes?' (the voice is jaded, sighing, – 'busy').

'My name is . . . , I'm the supply teacher.' You smile in the hope it will be returned. It isn't. Already you sense it will be an 'interesting' day.

'Look, I don't know what class you've got – ask the cleaner he normally knows what's going on around here.' (Actually the secretary doesn't say *that*, but for all the help she is she might as well have done.) She eventually finds out what class you've 'got' and time is ticking on. You want to find your classroom, or at least get the 'lay of the land' and focus for the day.

A brief visit to the staffroom and you notice the typically busy terminal between 'partial freedom' and 'professional responsibility'. A few teachers look your way. No one says 'Hi.' You say 'Good morning, I'm . . . ' as you approach a 'colleague' and ask where room 12A is, and get a hurried commiseration. 'You've got 7A . . . double period . . . watch your back . . . ' He hurries off.

Does this sound contrived? No – but fortunately it's not too common. Most schools, these days, are quite supportive of supply teachers.

You'll cope. You'll survive. You'll even teach! You're a supply teacher.

Chapter 2 outlines a different kind of typical day of supply teaching. Building on that case study in the subsequent chapters are the sorts of skills, approaches and necessary qualities that enable more effective (and enjoyable) supply teaching.

Being the professional

I have seen some supply teachers:

- who seem bent on doing the least amount of work possible for that day – *merely* 'supervising' not engaging, teaching, giving encouragement and feedback; in short not *being* a teacher;
- reading a novel while the class was effectively 'doing their own thing'. This teacher did not even flinch when I walked into 'her class'; she appeared oblivious to the reality that most of the class were skilfully off-task;
- sit in a high-school class using a personal mobile phone doing business that has nothing to do with their professional responsibilities for that class (and I'm not talking about emergency use of mobile phones here);
- doing work at the teacher's desk, that has, clearly, nothing to do with *that* lesson.

Thankfully I haven't seen too many supply teachers who will take good money yet behave as unprofessionally as this.

When we walk into a school as a supply teacher we have the same rights *and* obligations as our regular teaching peers. We don't have the benefit of having a longer-term role as our regular colleagues but we do not need to play down, minimize, apologize or excuse the fact we are teachers *here, today* . We need to relate to our collegial peers, students and parents as the professional. However, if we want to be treated as the professional we need to evidence those behaviours that will accord that normative status.

Some of the common concerns I hear from supply teachers include:

- I'm often concerned about what I might face with student behaviour whether or not I'll be able to 'handle things', whether or not I'll 'lose control'.
- I don't know their names, they sometimes give me false names and laugh and 'carry on'; it's not a good start.
- I feel like a glorified 'babysitter' in some schools, like I'm not taken seriously by other staff or even the students.
- I have to take so many different subjects; things I wasn't trained for like Art, Phys. Ed. even Music. (This secondary teacher, on the day in question, was trying his best to take a very restless group of students

for 'ball-handling' skills in the gym.)
• Going into a new class *every* day I teach, seeing a sea of new faces and
  not having any relationship with them at the outset and having to go
  through that 'testing-out' time.

I have worked with many supply teachers in Australia, New Zealand and
the UK in in-service education, professional development and mentoring
(one to one). In sharing the sorts of comments listed most supply teachers
are not negative about their role, just naturally anxious, aware of the
special challenges faced by going to new school settings each day or week.
There are times when we might even feel especially vulnerable, such as
when we are asked to take a known hard class; the year head frowns,

grimaces and swallows hard as they pass us the class list and pat us on the shoulder: '8D . . . do your best.'

The recurring concern that supply teachers commonly voice is that they want a genuine, practical, degree of colleague support (even for their brief 'tenure'). Their role is enhanced when they are acknowledged, affirmed and supported as a professional – as a *fellow teacher* – by their colleagues in their host schools.

All the examples and cases in this book are drawn from my mentoring work in Australian and British schools over the last five years. I have addressed the typical and normal concerns about behaviour management and discipline that always face 'supply' teachers. I have also addressed some of the more 'thorny' issues faced by supply teachers, such as very hard to manage classes and issues of harassment of teachers. I trust you will find the book practical, encouraging and enabling. I hope you will seek out the support options detailed in this book.

A supply teacher is not *merely* or *just* a supply teacher, he or she is an indispensable member, a professional member, of any colleague team in any school. It is crucially important that our profession acknowledges and supports supply teachers as fellow professionals. How supply teachers are treated by their full-time collegial peers also depends on how the supply teachers perceive their role in schools; how they professionally carry themselves; how they carry out their professional obligations as a teacher – on any given day, week or term.

Chapter 7 outlines how schools can more actively, consciously, support supply teachers within their school; how they can enable their supply colleague more effectively to engage their professional role in their school.

The issue of 'colleague watchfulness' is developed in this text with special reference to a supply teacher plan that advocates school-wide expectations for supply teacher colleagues.

2

A normal teaching day?: A case example of supply teaching

You come most carefully upon your hour.

(Shakespeare, *Hamlet, I: i*)

Liz Smith is a supply teacher in her mid-thirties; she's back teaching (after a break for family commitments). She enjoys a few days' teaching, in different schools most weeks; sometimes she gets several straight days at one school. She's had an early morning call from the 'supply provider'. Sometimes she gets the call the night before. Today she's got a grade 6.

Liz gets to school early – East London. She has not taught in this particular school before. It's 8.15 a.m. She knows how important it is to get to a school early; paperwork, directions, check out the classroom, get focused etc. She parks in a place far from any spot that looks like it is reserved, or those that the regular teachers will want to use. (It's just early 'protocol'.)

She unpacks her 'gear' – a large plastic tub and a bag. She has brought the normal supply teacher's 'kit': extra pens, rulers, pencils and paper; chalk, duster and whiteboard markers just in case (she's been caught before); a range of user-friendly worksheets (just in case – for 'early finishers' and the few 'bored' students); several 'largish' laminated rule-posters outlining, in bold colourful lettering, the basic rules she'll remind the class of at the outset of the day. She's even brought her own cup (not as a 'Linus blanket' but another just-in-case 'protocol'). At one school, some years back, she'd gone into the staff room at morning tea, reached for a cup from the shelf and some miserable person had said 'That's *my* cup!' She felt like telling her to . . . She didn't, she 'apologized'.

'What kind of class will I have?' Liz muses as she heads for the administration. She knows she's got 11–12-year-olds (grade 6); she's a little anxious (naturally) she hasn't worked at this school before. As a supply teacher she's had a wide range of classes – mostly at the hard-to-manage end of the distribution through to the 'lunatic' (she rarely goes back to those schools).

The office secretary is inviting, helpful – she welcomes her and hands her a 'pack'. Smiling she says, 'I'm sure you've seen one of these before?' The 'pack' contains a user-friendly map of the school, the names of the teachers and their respective classes, the specialist teachers and aides (some schools even include small photos of staff). The bell times (recess) and assembly times are set out along with the day's timetable. 'I've written in your photocopy number for the day.' Dropping her voice she adds, 'Limit 60 . . . OK? Cheers.' The secretary points out that her ' "teaching buddy" – we couldn't really think what else to call them – for today is Carmel Brown (6B) she'll probably be in the staffroom or her class. She'll take you to her room, show you round, be on hand. Hope you have a good day with 6D.'

Off to the staffroom (the map helps) where she sees several teachers having an early cuppa and a chat; one approaches, welcomes her to the school and introduces her to the others.

'Have you got Paula's class?'

'Paula?'

'Paula Davies, 6D.'

'Oh yes.'

One of the teachers gives a wry grin, 'I wish you the best . . . Watch out for Troy.' The speaker heads off to her class. (How many Troys, Nathans and Melissas has she been warned to 'watch out for' since taking up supply teaching? One of the other teachers notes, 'They're not that bad really. Who's your teaching buddy?' They chat for a while and Carmel Brown (teaching buddy) comes in, walks over and introduces herself. Liz goes down the corridor with her colleague to yet another class. It isn't always this welcoming, this supportive. She's learned to take the rough with the smooth.

She checks with her colleague about any particular routines she needs to be aware of with the grade 6s.

• Do they line up before coming into class; how?

- Any special seating plan?
- Any particular ways their regular teacher gets whole-class attention? (p. 58).

School-wide routines are noted in the support teacher's pack. Her support colleague runs through the 'time-out plan' – 'just in case'. (This too is listed in 'the kit plan'. The first 'time-out' port-of-call is the teaching buddy's classroom.)

'All the best, Liz.'

Carmel moves into her class next to Liz's classroom for the day; it's 8.30 a.m. She scans the room, checks out the seating arrangements (rows), resource books and class pets (just goldfish). It is a bright, attractive (if old) classroom environment. It 'feels' OK – *she now has to make it OK.*

The teacher's desk is quite tidy; it's not always the case. In some classrooms she has worked in it looks somewhat like a tip. She sometimes can't find the class roll, or any set-work, or the set-work that is left is ambiguous or minimalist ('revise work on Tudor houses . . . ' 'Revise pattern and order . . . ' 'Check all spelling lists . . . ' – What spelling lists?). On those days her personal armoury of work topics, worksheets, activities and games always comes in handy and often gives the students a 'novelty-break' from their normal 'fare'.

The regular teacher has left some set-work in a folder on the teacher's desk. She notes that the first period includes literacy, a full grammar revision (with lesson framework) on prepositions. There are some worksheets to extend the class discussion. 'Hmmm . . . prepositions?' – she gets an idea and decides that a quick visit to the infant department might help. She notices that there are no rules posted up anywhere in the classroom – well it's term three.

Liz quickly puts up her three rule-posters – blu-tacked to the chalkboard. Their language is positive, concise, behavioural:

To learn well here:
- we put our hand up in question/discussion time,
- we use our 'partner-voices' inside,
- if we need teacher assistance we . . .

To show respect here we:

To feel safe here we: (see pp. 68–70)

At 8.55 a.m. she hears the first bell – the reminder/warning bell for

students to come in from the playground (or wherever) to class. This school has a 'lining-up' policy; Liz goes to the classroom door.

She's aware that some of the class will be a little anxious at the arrival of the 'new' teacher; she'll be 'different'. Some students will be naturally inquisitive. 'Will she be strict?' 'Nice?' 'Nasty?' 'A pushover?' 'Will she have a sense of humour?' 'What kind of work will we do?' She knows that the students will be asking such questions as soon as they see her at the door. Some of the students, she knows, will actively test her mettle. 'What can we get away with today?' (She's used to that.)

A few students run up and brake sharply at room 15's classroom door. 'Where's Ms Davies?' Another adds, 'You gunna be our teacher?' Another adds provocatively: 'You're not our teacher!' ('Is that Troy?' she wonders). She doesn't answer these questions, she gives a general answer to them all. 'I'm Ms Smith. Your regular teacher is away today. I'll be taking your class.'

She is pleasant but she won't start mini-discussions now, outside the classroom. She'll give the full introduction later. She scans the restless group in a rough semblance of 'a line', and says, 'Settling down, everyone.' She pauses to give some take-up time. The bulk of the students have arrived. 'Troy' says, 'When we going in?' (Poor chap has been standing outside his classroom for 40 seconds.) Another adds, 'Yeah, what you doing here, Miss – you going to be our teacher?' (Troy's mate has an attentionally sing-song voice.) She *tactically* ignores this comment. She sees them settle, she adds, 'My name is Ms Smith, I'll be taking 6D today while Ms Davies is away . . . Before we go in, folks – remember we're going into a classroom; I notice a few hats and coats still on. Thanks.'

This descriptive reminder is a conscious preference over merely telling them (e.g. 'Take your hats and coats off') or asking 'why': 'Why have you got your hats on when we're clearly going into a classroom?' 'Why are you head-butting him down the back there?' (to two lads down the back of the line who are playfully punching each other). Instead she lifts her voice and says: 'Boys, playtime's over – we're going into class.' (Sometimes she'll add 'We keep our hands and feet to ourselves here'.)

'When we go in,' she adds, 'please sit quietly in your regular seats. Thanks. Off we go.'

She opens the door, stands aside and greets them, smiling, as they come in. If any push or shove she'll direct them to 'stand aside for a moment – thanks', adding 'In our class we come in without pushing and shoving.' Her tone is clear; she is defining (briefly) a purposeful entry to class. If she lets them just barge in, noisily, coats and hats still on, pushing and shoving it will make the next 10 minutes that more difficult. She knows that how a teacher establishes entry to a classroom is crucial – it's a defining part of the lesson or day.

The class files in, (just a few minutes of the day have passed!) Some slump in their seats (Troy?), some return her smile, most sense a 'businesslike' start. Liz waits for the group to initially settle. She stands at the front of the room, scanning the faces, now and then making brief eye-contact (a few look away). She looks relaxed, expectant of their co-operation. Her body language is 'open' (no folded arms, no dropped head or tense frowning). With a restless class she often cues the expectation of whole-class attention and focus by a verbal cue: 'Settling down', with a brief tactical pause to allow take-up, adding 'Eyes and ears this way, thanks.' She's learned that whenever she gives management directions it helps to *focus on expected behaviour* instead of focusing merely on the negative behaviours: 'You shouldn't be talking should you?' (Not a helpful question!) She also knows that standing with her arms folded, tapping her foot ('I'm waiting, *thank you!*') or pacing up and down while trying to get attention ('You're too noisy! Be quiet!') only telegraphs corresponding motoric restlessness in those students with 'undiagnosed ADD' (attention deficit disorder)!

She is aware of her general body language; her manner, her tone of voice. She is not an 'actor' but she is aware she needs to project a confident teacher-leadership where she is seen to be sure, in herself, in her role. As they settle she briefly acknowledges those students who are attending, and listening ('Thanks') as she makes scanning eye-contact.

Confidence

She is aware that the way she 'presents' (comes across) needs to look, and sound, confident. While naturally anxious at times (with some of the secondary classes she has taken) she knows these are students – children and young people. She knows they respond to confident, positive, relaxed leadership. She smiles often; her relaxed and positive demeanour and spatial presence often – almost always – sees a positive correspondence in her students.

Her 'dress' (she would rather dress 'up' than 'down') befits her role; she has seen supply teachers who appear to have no regard for any sense of reasonable professional dress. She looks 'smart' (without overdoing it; she is aware – in part – that clothes 'maketh' . . .). She looks as if she means business – the business of teaching.

They are 'settled' now; a few are leaning back a little languorously in their seats (she *tactically* ignores that for now). A few are leaning back in their seats; she gives some brief eye-contact to those students adding, 'Four on the floor with your seats, thanks.' Again her tone is pleasant and expectant as she quickly reclaims whole-class attention. She 'formally' begins: 'Good morning again; as I said outside our classroom just before my name is . . . '

A few students start to 'gas-bag' to each other while Ms Smith is addressing the class. She pauses. The students in question look up. She asks them their names then describes their behaviour 'Crystal, Tiffany, Elisa,' Ms Smith *tactically* ignores the sibilant sigh of Elisa. 'You're talking, I'm trying to speak to our class.' She already starts to use some inclusive language (*'our* class'). She sometimes adds a brief *simple direction* to the descriptive comment e.g. 'Looking this way and listening, thanks.' Again her voice tone *sounds* as if in addressing their behaviour it is no 'big deal'; she is keeping the flow and tenor of her discipline 'least intrusive'. She has learned to direct students to expected *behaviour* using action phrases (verbs/participles), e.g.: 'Hands up without calling out.' 'Looking this way, thanks.' She is conscious not to use 'requests' (e.g. *'Would you mind* putting your hand up to ask a question?').

Liz resumes the flow of the lesson quickly. If a student is cockily rude, calling out silly or provocative comments, she will firmly, briefly, assert: 'That kind of comment is unacceptable (even totally unacceptable) in our classroom' (p. 33) or 'I don't speak to you like that I don't expect you to speak to me rudely' or 'We've got a class rule for respect. I expect you to use it.'

She is aware that when she needs to use an assertive tone or manner she avoids any hostile or aggressive tones: pointing, gesticulating fingers, overly raised voice (as distinct from a firm voice; replete with serious intent). She has learned to briefly, specifically, *describe* what it is that is offensive in the student's behaviour, and assert that such behaviour is unacceptable. She then continues without holding grudges (the hardest part!); she appears unthreatened by some of these young 'cocksparrows'.

On rare occasions she has had to direct a student to leave the classroom and take time-out – to go to a 'set place' or 'person' as nominated in the school's time-out policy (pp. 89–93). As she marks the class roll a few students give false names. She has already said it will take a while to learn their names; she'll 'do her best with their help'. 'Each time I speak to you personally, even in whole-class discussion please give me your name.' (She's learned Troy's name already and Crystal, Tiffany and Elisa). One of the students responds to the roll call with a name that evokes laughter. She suspects the 'game' adding, 'You've either got a humourous name or you're using two names. I'm sure you didn't mean to make it difficult for me?' She leaves it at that and moves on. One lad uses a girl's name (to giggles). Ms Smith pauses, and says in a firm whisper, 'When you've remembered your real name let me know.'

Her straight-faced, pleasant, repartee is returned with the lad raising his eyes to the ceiling, and giving a wry grin. She moves on – keeping 'the flow'.

A student walks in late. He's surprised to see a different teacher: 'Who are you?'

'My name is Ms Smith, welcome to our class; what's your name?'

'Kent,' (he frowns, a bit suspicious).

'You're late,' she says this merely as an acknowledgement, she is pleasant – smiling. She doesn't ask *why* he's late (at this stage in the lesson). All she is doing is *redefining the moment* by 'stopping him', acknowledging what is occurring (his lateness) and directing him to a seat. She has seen other teachers let students walk in five minutes late, walk past their teacher (ignoring the fact that they're talking to the class), and the student then starts chatting to a few classmates as they take their seat behaving as if the teacher doesn't exist.

'Kent, there's a couple of seats by the window, thanks.' She gives a brief incidental 'direction'. As she reclaims the flow of speaking to the class group, taking her eyes off him, he says, 'But I sit with Adam and Craig down the back there.' He points to the back row. Ms Smith has no idea if he normally sits there; anyway all the back row is 'filled' and she is not going to have the drama of a big seat rearrangement now (she *may* do that later). She is well aware that confronting language is counter-productive (e.g. 'I don't care who you sit with, I said sit there!')

She *partially* acknowledges what he's said (she's learned that this avoids most counter-challenge) and redirects, 'Those seats down the back are taken – for now there are spare seats by the window. Thanks, Kent.'

She beckons him to move across to that seat. He shuffles off; wry mouth, rocking his head (is he trying to say something? Probably). Ms Smith is *tactically* ignoring the student's body language and quiet mutter. Her eyes are now, quickly, back on 'her class group' and she reclaims the 'flow' of the establishment of the day's activity.

'Before we start any of our lessons today, you'll have noticed I've got some posters on the board here. They are the classroom rules I'll be using with you today. I know your regular teacher, Ms Davies, has rules with you. I've checked with the principal and, as you'll see, these rules are almost the same as those Ms Davies made with you back in August.'

If at any point a student calls out or butts in she will point back to the rule-poster as a visible reminder, and may add, 'Remember our rule for asking questions/or for class discussion, thanks.' Some calling out behaviour she will *tactically* ignore, but if it is repeated she will direct the individual, or whole-class, to 'remember our rule'. The rule-posters address three core rights: *the right to learn* (without disruption or unfair distraction); *the right to feel safe*; *the right to have one's person/property treated with respect* (no put-downs, teasing) and highlight the basic, fair, responsibilities that flow from those rights.

OUR LEARNING RULE:
We all have a right to learn:
- this means we have expected materials,
- give learning time our best shot,
- hands up (without calling out),
- partner-voice and co-operative talk (in class learning time).
OUR SAFETY RULE (covers behaviours like appropriate movement, use of equipment, keep hands and feet to yourself).
OUR RESPECT RULE (covers behaviours like personal space, property of class and other class members, use of language [not put-downs, cheap shots, swearing]).

She holds up a small, fluffy toy rabbit and starts the first formal lesson for the day (prepositions).

The novelty of the rabbit sees smiles and mild surprise on the faces: 'What's all this then?' She takes the rabbit to the board writing the word 'preposition'.

Facing the class she says, 'I've a box here and a rabbit – haven't named him yet. He's stuffed, I mean (she winks) he's a stuffed toy.' (She'd raced down to the infant department to get a toy animal before class time.) 'This rabbit's home today is this box. I'll need a volunteer to help him home.' A dozen hands shoot up. Several students call out 'Me!' 'Can I come up?' Stating the obvious, yet again, she says, 'A number of students are calling out.' (She is careful not to say 'all' students.) 'Remember our class rule,' (she points briefly to the poster), ' "Hands up without calling out". Thanks.' She'll have to reinforce this fair expectation (via the rule) several times – patiently. She knows it's important not to simply accept calling out (even with hands up).

Several hands stay up, she numbers them off, '1, 2, 3 . . . You can put your hands down, I'll remember. Ta.' One of the boys calls out quickly, several times 'Me, me, me, me,'. The teacher holds up a 'blocking-hand' (palm out). He stops – their eyes meet across the room, every student obviously listening in – 'I thought your name was Daniel not Mimi.'

'What?' (He doesn't immediately get the dry wit.)

'Mimi?' (me me, me me)

'Oh – yeah.'

She adds, 'Hands up and I'll listen, Daniel.' She drops eye-contact and resumes the flow of instructional time.

She chooses a student – Mandy. 'Now, Mandy, a bit of help for the rabbit. First – he needs a name.' Mandy chooses 'Heath'.

'So, Mandy, how will Heath get *into* the box, or *on* the box or, maybe, – *under* the box?'

Using the unusual, kinaesthetic, novelty (the rabbit) she develops the key elements in this unit of work: the main nouns, 'box' and 'rabbit'; the key verbs 'jumps', 'hops', 'crawls' and the prepositions 'in', 'on', 'over', 'near', 'by' etc.

Mandy chooses a preposition and – several students later – the main concept is sinking in as the words build on the board. She then extends the language. 'What kind of rabbit? Fat? Lazy? Big? Small?' One of the boys (Daniel) suggests that 'his' rabbit, 'Fritz', 'waltzed' 'towards' 'the box'. 'Has Fritz been watching *Neighbours*?' she smiles at him. Students contribute to a more involved and extended sentence structure that forms the basis for the on-task phase of the lesson.

One of the boys, Troy, asks if he can go to the toilet. As she is still in the middle of whole-class teaching she gives a conditional direction: 'When I've finished class teaching time I'll organize a toilet break.' She has learned that a 'conditional' direction ('when/then') nearly always meets a co-operative response.

She never asks a student 'why' they want to go to the toilet 'now' or 'why didn't you go at recess time?' Nor does she simply say, 'No, you can't.' She knows a straight negative (on a toilet request) can easily create unnecessary conflict.

On occasions (in other schools, mostly secondary) she had a few students 'demand' to go to the toilet (during whole-class instructional time). 'I'm desperate for a pee Miss – desperate!' On such occasions she lets them go but keeps a careful record of time and how long. She always checks the school's 'release from class' policy (as it varies across schools; p. 119).

Ms Smith clarifies the set learning task and the key worksheets for 'learning-task-time'. Before she finishes the whole-class phase of the lesson she clarifies the importance of 'partner-voice' – co-operative talk (talk that doesn't focus on *Neighbours* or *Home and Away*; how to get her assistance and appropriate movement around the room.

She discusses with them the meaning of 'partner-voice' inviting their understanding. 'Remember . . . there's 28 of us in here; a small room, a lot of voices, we need to make the effort: 'soft voice', 'eye-contact', 'speaking with the person next to you – not *the student three seats away.*' She smiles as she emphasizes this point.

While the noise level of students' voices and normal movement will naturally rise during on-task learning time, she will verbally, and non-verbally, cue the class if group noise gets too loud. She will also encourage individuals when they make the effort to use a quiet, working voice. Sometimes she will non-verbally cue to a few students by indicating 'volume turn-down'. She consciously makes an effort to keep any corrective discipline encouraging and positive and to keep the emphasis on teaching and learning.

During the on-task phase of the lesson, Ms Smith circulates around the room to encourage, give feedback, refocus off-task students, help etc. She's learned that it is important to circulate rather than sit at her desk and seek to 'manage' from there. She notices a couple of students sitting, doing nothing, turning around talking (and distracting) other students. She says, 'I notice you're not working' (she describes what they *are* doing). She's about to add the question designed to encourage some responsibility (e.g. 'What are you supposed to be doing now?') when one of the students says: 'I haven't got a pen.' The other student says. 'My pencil case was stolen from my locker.'

She's been caught before on this one. Rather than ask why they haven't got pens or rulers (or whatever), she alerts them to access her yellow box. 'See that box over there (she points to the 10″ × 4″ × 4″ box). There's pens in there – red and blue pens.' The student whinges, 'Yeah, but I haven't got a ruler or any paper.' 'There's paper lined and plain next to the box, and rulers in the box.' The student mutters 'Shit.' The teacher adds a quiet parting aside, 'There's none of that in the box, there are pens and rulers.' She 'leaves', giving him take-up time and a quiet, implied, task reminder, 'I'll be back.' Each ruler, pen, pencil has a tip of yellow tape (visible). Some supply colleagues often put their names on the pens, etc. Other supply colleagues lend the pens and record the student's name in a 'loan book'. Either way it is thinking preventatively rather that reacting to events as they come. (She's learned to avoid asking 'why' a student doesn't have appropriate, necessary, equipment. That only ends in 'avoidance', 'excusing' or arguing (p. 30, 48).

A couple of boys are playing with small toys, half doing their work. Ms Smith suspects these boys may not be working too well together. She muses about the possibility of directing them to work separately (there are a few spare desks).

She goes over and asks to see their work. 'Hello boys, let me try to remember your names. How's the work going? Let's have a look.'

She is conscious of using 'proximity' and 'personal space' thoughtfully. She doesn't pick up the students' work without basic courtesies such as 'I'd like to have a look at your work, thanks.' 'Can I have a look?', 'How's it going then?' 'Do you mind if I write the correct spelling in the margin?'

She has a brief task-focused chat with the boys ('What are you supposed to be doing now?'). Her tone is pleasant, inquiring, positively focused on the work requirement. As she begins to move away she turns and says, quietly, 'Michael . . . I want you to put those Harry Potter toys in your desk or you can leave them on my table until recess'.

He protests he wasn't playing with them. She replies, 'Even if you weren't, I want you to put . . . ' (she repeats the directed choice). She knows that *simply* taking a student's personal toy, or trinket, will probably result in an unnecessary, and pointless, power struggle. Whenever she has given a student a directed choice ('in your desk or on my table') she hasn't yet had a student put their *objet d'art* on the teacher's table. On occasions where students refuse to put distracting objects away she will make the consequences clear through a deferred consequence (see p. 86, 87). She will not get drawn into power struggles.

The two students get back to work; slowly. There are a few sighs which she tactically ignores (p. 41f). She exercises a lot of conscious, *tactical*, ignoring, which keeps the flow, and focus, of her leadership on the main issue of teaching and learning.

Later in the lesson she comes across to the two boys to 're-establish' the working relationship with them (at their desks). She is pleasant; neither condescending or recriminating. She gives some brief, descriptive feedback, 'Aaron ... you've completed that section on the common prepositions – that's an interesting use of adverb there in the way you've described how your rabbit jumped onto the box "immediately". What made him jump immediately?'

When Liz encourages her students she is conscious to:
- keep the focus on their effort, energy and contribution rather than to *globally* praise – 'That's great', 'marvellous', 'fantastic', 'brilliant'. These global words, as such, give no feedback about *what* was 'great', 'brilliant' or 'wonderful' etc.
- not qualify her encouragement/feedback e.g. 'You've written several thoughtful sentences here. *If you'd done that when I asked earlier in the lesson I wouldn't have had to remind you half a dozen times would I?'*
- to keep the encouragement 'private' (as it were) and not 'loudly' hold up a student's work and remark on it. As students get older they tend not to respond too positively to 'public praise' when the focus is academic feedback.

She is consciously aware of even *basic* posture reinforcement such as a smile, even a brief verbal acknowledgement, 'That's it', 'You've got it', 'That's right', 'Well done', 'You're on the right track'; an *appropriate* touch on the arm/shoulder when the student is back on task. 'That's it, Jonathan, you've set out the work plan, well done . . . Now what do you need to do next?'

This brief 'connecting reinforcement ' is very important, particularly if we have had to discipline a student earlier in the lesson. Even just coming back to the student's workplace to acknowledge, affirm and to give task feedback can be a form of re-establishing those normative working relationships between teacher and student. It is important, though, not to *discount* any positive reinforcement given, i.e.: 'You've started very well, yes that's how to link the noun and the verb . . . *now if you had done that the first time instead of wasting time like I said before then you would have got much more work done, wouldn't you?'*

She continues to rove around the classroom; scanning, generally encouraging individuals, re-forming, clarifying, giving feedback and brief written comments where necessary.

If students have trouble working together, she will make the consequences of their task-avoidance, and distracting behaviour, clear to them through a 'choice': 'If you continue to keep distracting each other by talking I'll have to ask you to work separately – think about it. 'She will then move off and leave the consequences of their 'choice' with them. She will not brook discussion of the veracity of their protestations or their whining discounting – 'Gees, Miss, others talk and that as well!'

The most disruptive incident she has had today was with Troy. She had had a few 'run-ins' before recess when he had been wandering around during the on-task phase of the lesson hassling some of his 'class-mates'.

Having directed him back to his seat for the third time ('What are you supposed to be doing now Troy?' she had asked quietly, but firmly) he kicked a chair, it fell over and he swore (not at Ms Smith but at 'the ether'). 'F___!! Can't do nothing in here!! F—-ing do nothing.' She had been warned that Troy sometimes 'loses it'.

At this point in the lesson she directs him to leave 'our classroom'.

'Troy, I've asked you to settle down and work by the fair rules. You've continued to . . . ' (Here be *brief* and *specific* about the student's behaviour.) 'It's better you leave now.' (She resists the temptation to add 'before I snot you one!') She's doing her best to keep 'calm', assertive by 'calm') 'Go to . . . ', (the time-out option). 'I'll get together with you later to see how we can work things out.'

He walks out, pushing the door loudly, adding an *ex parte* 'Shit!' She doesn't comment on this but resumes the flow of the lesson. She will follow up with him at lunch recess. The policy at this school is that each department has nominated colleagues they can send a student to for 'time-out' (p. 89ff).

She welcomes him back (after lunch) having had a talk with him for 10 minutes at lunch time with the deputy head. No recriminations but a positive reminder about what is expected after lunch recess (p. 87ff).

The bell will go soon – Liz has set her watch alarm for five minutes before first recess. She cues the whole-class for class attention (by 'tinging' a small glass with her pen).

'Eyes and ears this way . . . Thanks . . . ' She waits for them to process the whole-class direction. She is aware that if she starts talking over their natural working noise, or through it, it will only reinforce to the students that it is 'OK to talk while the teacher is up the front talking to us'. She waits for them to settle, cueing the half dozen individuals still working or 'chatting'. 'A number of students are still working. Dean, Siobhan, Hanady . . . Eyes and ears this way . . . Paul . . . Troy . . . Pens down. Thanks.'

She will not talk to the whole class, or give closure and exit directions, *until* they are all attending. She knows how easy it is to reinforce that pattern of behaviour where students are only half-listening, half-chatting *while* the teacher is talking. Even if she is 'only' here – at this school – for a day she wants to reinforce positive teacher leadership (she may be back!).

There are five minutes to go before recess. She has a quick whole-class recap of the lesson on prepositions, reinforcing they key ideas and skills of this unit of work. Any student who calls out she will *tactically* ignore, if they call out a second time she will give a positive, brief, rule reminder, 'Travis . . . remember hand up. Thanks.' Then, at that point, she will acknowledge any other students with their hands up (who are not calling out).

'Alright before we go out to recess a few reminders *for us all* . . . in a moment I want you to straighten the furniture, a quick tidy-up: pick up any litter off the floor, *off* . . . That's another preposition (off) and drop it *in* the bin on your way *out* (two more prepositions; they're everywhere). Thanks. Also, chairs *behind* the desks and we'll leave row by row.' A few students sigh (she tactically ignores this). 'Siobhan, your row first . . . Carmen, your row second, Travis, your row last.' She is well aware that this brief, prefacing, reminder is basic, but important. She has seen whole classes race out noisily where teachers do not clarify and enforce that expectation.

The bell goes. The first row leaves. As they do a couple of boys in the front row try to 'duck out'. 'Michael . . . Sean . . . back behind your chairs.' They sigh and click their tongues – 'Gees . . . it's recess.' The second row leaves. As they do she says to Michael and Sean, 'I want to see you for a couple of minutes after class.' 'What for?' Michael whines. Michael pushes his chair hard against his desk; Sean mutters loudly, 'Can't do nothing here with her!' 'Two minutes,' she says as she turns away from them and directs the last row out.

Michael and Sean stay back sulkily leaning against the wall. Approaching them she says, 'I know you're probably annoyed that I've asked you to stay back for a couple of minutes.' She is not angry with them, she is pleasant but decisive.

'Yeah well, we didn't do anything – what do we have to stay in for?'

'I've asked you stay back only to remind you about our class rule for respect. Michael . . . Sean . . . I'm concerned about you trying to rush off before the bell and then getting uptight, kicking your chairs and saying what you did, Sean ("Can't do nothing with her"). I won't speak disrespectfully to you so I don't expect you to speak disrespectfully about me.'

'It's not fair – the bell's gone,' whines Michael. She partially agrees, 'You're right, the bell had gone. In our class though the bell is a reminder for the class that class learning time is over – it's my job to dismiss the class (direct you all to leave). You two tried to beat the bell, eh?' (She smiles at them.) Boys – it's only a few minutes past the bell, that's all. I want you to enjoy the rest of playtime *and* the rest of our day together. OK?'

Michael and Sean reluctantly return a wry and jaded smile. She makes a conscious effort to finish this brief after-class chat as amicably as possible.

This brief follow-up has not taken long and the rest of the class will soon pick up the 'tribal tom-toms' re: the fact that this new teacher does not simply 'let things go'.

The boys wander off to recess. Ms Smith tidies up and heads off for a cup of tea.

As the day progresses she is conscious that the class are slowly 'getting used to her' and getting used to her 'style' and leadership approach. They are realizing that although she is decisive, and at times assertive, she is positive and encouraging in her feedback and general manner towards them. Her teaching has been largely enjoyable, and she has sought to keep them on-task at all times. To those few students who have engaged in task-avoiding behaviour she made the consequential options clear: 'If you choose not to do the work now I'll have to ask you to stay back and complete it at recess.' She is always sensitive to the possibility that some students will have problems with the work. She will always adjust or modify task expectations with students and obviously so for students with special needs (something she checked with the grade leader that day). What she doesn't do is bargain, or 'plead' with the students: 'Well what work *do* you want to do then?'

A few students had moaned that 'This work was boring'. Rather than defend 'her work' she will acknowledge (sometimes with humour) that work can be boring sometimes but 'It is the work that we've all been doing today. How can I help you get it done more enjoyably?'

She has had students (in some schools) blatantly refuse to engage in the set learning task (or modified learning tasks). Rather than argue, or threaten, again she makes the consequences clear – *deferred* consequences. If she has a student say 'I don't care' she points out positively, briefly and firmly that she cares and then gives the student take-up time. If they in any way begin to interfere with other students' learning time she will give the 'choice' to stay and work by the fair rules or be directed away (out of the class) for time-out. At all times she avoids getting drawn into an 'argumentative' scenario, making clear, briefly, that their behaviour is 'their choice'.

Often, in such cases, the student's behaviour is an expression (perhaps a normative expression) of attentional or power-seeking behaviour ('I can do what I want and you can't stop me!'). It is unreasonable to expect a supply teacher to engage in the longer-term counselling support that the regular teacher would normally be engaged in. Supply teachers should be expected to teach, lead and discipline professionally and positively, and enjoy 'no blame' back-up when that small percentage of recidivist students effectively 'holds a class to ransom'.

By and large the day has gone well. As the clock winds towards 3.30 p.m. she is aware she needs to allow for pack-up, tidy-up and last feedback/marking for the afternoon session. She has had some 'fun' word games in the last 20 minutes, to finish with a more relaxed session.

She makes sure there is a monitor to hand out the 'notices' for that day. She reminds the class that the bell will be going soon – five minutes. 'Let's do the cleaner a favour. Last bits of litter off the floor, chairs on the

table. Thanks for tidying your desks so quickly. Remember, too, we leave row by row. Sean and Michael, your row first – walking (in two minutes).' She thanks them for their support as a class group this day.

'I've enjoyed my time with you all. I wish you all the best. You never know I may meet you again.' She scans the room as the school bell sounds, beckoning Sean's row to go. She has chats with a few individuals as they leave. Some come up to thank her. In *some* schools children have come up to her privately and asked her if *she* can be their *normal* teacher. ('Can you come and be our teacher all the time, Miss?'). She has a chat with the few parents who have come to pick their children up.

Liz makes sure she leaves the classroom tidy. If the teacher's desk is 'chaotically messy' (it is in some schools) she is careful to leave the class roll in another prominent place (rather than tidy the teacher's desk in a way that might add insult to injury – she has been in some classrooms that seem to have an entrenched 'pig-sty' aesthetic).

She leaves a note explaining what she has covered that day and a brief, positive, comment on any students she has had to follow through with regarding time-out procedures (p. 89ff).

Liz hops into her car, having said goodbye to the head teacher (when she can find her/him). As she drives out of the car park she reflects, again, that today wasn't too bad. 'I even enjoyed myself at times.' She muses, briefly, that some of the students might remember what a preposition is (or at least how a 'rabbit' can move in relation to a box!).

There are many supply teachers like Liz in the profession. They do much more than simply 'cover' a class: they teach. Such teachers are invaluable to the profession of teaching, they support both their colleagues and, of course, the students. Over a day, or more, they enable a class (and a school) to be what they exist for – a workable, even enjoyable, learning community.

3

Assertion, confidence and teacher leadership

It is excellent to have a giant's strength but it is tyrannous to use it like a giant.

(Shakespeare, *Measure for Measure, II: ii*)

The most common whinge heard from students by supply teachers is the 'teacher comparison whinge': 'Mr/Ms Smith lets us chew gum; eat in class, read comics (when we've done our work); sit wherever we like; choose what work we want, dance on the tables . . . ' Arguing about the relative truthfulness of any of this is a waste of time as it is overly defending what you – as supply teacher – will do in comparison to their probable 'fiction', or at least their heavily 'doctored' version of normal reality in their classroom.

If our rules and routines are fair (p. 68ff) and if we have made an effort to correlate what we do with what the regular teacher normally does (regarding behaviour and learning), we will be doing our reasonable, and professional, best.

It is also important to be aware (we'll soon find out!) that children who are 'difficult', or even challenging, may well be so for their regular teachers as well. Annoying and unpleasant as it may be, some children in *some* schools, will 'fool around', 'argue', 'challenge' and even 'bait' their supply teachers just as they annoyingly do for their regular teachers.

Such students can, on occasions, even manage to engage other students to collude with them in 'having fun' with their 'new teacher' (such is the 'discounting mentality' of such students – 'we're only having a bit of fun'). The degree to which a support teacher is able to refocus such potential behaviour depends on:

- prepared and positive rules and routines to take into classes (age-related p. 68ff);

- a personal discipline plan (Chapter 4);
- conscious planning for their supply teaching role – planning core lesson (generative) materials that do not depend on whether the class teacher has left clear, teachable, work; and, most of all,
- conscious support from colleagues in every school they work in (Chapter 7).

Supply teachers have to define *their* leadership with every class they teach as if it is a new class *for them*. While they can resource the regular teacher's rules, routines, classroom organization and 'lessons', supply teachers have to quickly, and confidently, define the classroom situation at the outset as their class, that day. The skills of positive management are crucial to that end as is the establishing of one's authority in a relaxed, but confidently assertive way, as is necessary.

The 25–30 individual students are an unknown quantity – as yet. Supply teachers know they must quickly engage and build a workable relationship with the class.

Confidence and authority

Students – even very young students – sense quickly how confident we are in our role as teacher-leaders. The way we *characteristically* come across in manner, tone of voice and body language; the things we say to engage, motivate, enthuse, manage or discipline all signal how assured we are with our authority to lead, teach and manage.

The students quickly tune-in to how confident we sound and look when we direct a class to 'line up', 'take coats off', 'face this way and listen', when we give typical discipline cues such as 'Remember the rule for . . . ', 'I want everyone looking this way and listening, thanks'. What they listen to is not merely our words – what we say – but our manner and bearing, the degree of confident (even relaxed) assertion in our voice, the way we scan the room, tactically, pausing to emphasize a point, to allow the processing of directions or reminders in our discipline. They 'read' us as *newcomers*, already having some conception of what a supply teacher can be like. In this there is the natural testing some students will exercise, or 'mete out', to supply teachers – this is par for the course.

In those first meetings we need to be able to *be* the teacher; not to evidence 'fear' at having to manage *this* class. You can tell some supply teachers 'by their oppressed and fear surprised eyes' (*Hamlet*, I: ii). There will be *natural* anxiety as we walk through the gates of some of our schools. Why wouldn't there be? It isn't a matter of merely sublimating our anxiety but remembering to *be* the teacher – the bona fide teacher who doesn't have to apologize or be deferent about 'only' being a supply teacher. We'll give them their money's worth today!

Our authority

Our authority is often expressed though our confidence – a confidence that resides in:

- our ability to engage, build and sustain rapport through a tone of purposefulness – why we are here together, today, doing *this* activity together;
- our general warmth – even appropriate humour – is responded to quickly by children. A sense we care (even if we're 'only' here for a day!) about this time together. Demonstrating such basic 'warmth' it is

not inconsistent with the need to exercise positive, and respectful, discipline where necessary;

- our ability to engage some attention and motivation in the learning for *that* period – some basic sense of worth in 'what we're doing today'. Often a supply teacher can entail some 'novel', 'fun', teaching as well as the prosaic learning tasks we have to teach;
- our ability to be sensitive to the appropriateness of the learning activity, or task, and catering for the visual, as well as auditory, learners (p. 15ff).

In all this our authority rests not so much in our stated role ('I *am* a teacher') but is based in our effective teaching and management. Displays of coercive, or authoritarian, 'power' have a short 'shelf-life' (even in a single day's teaching).

Behaving as if we *have* authority is about confidently behaving as a teacher-leader in ways that are likely to invite co-operation in our students (rather than trying to *prove* we have authority by a loud voice, bossy manner, use of threats, etc.) This requires some prior planning and a conscious management/discipline plan. This plan is based in a repertoire of teacher skills not merely resorting to the fact that 'I am a teacher' but 'What kind of teacher do I want to be?'

This may all sound patently obvious, yet I have seen many supply teachers – in practice – who expect to have their 'authority' accepted when they are clearly ill-prepared, do not make the effort to get to class on time, do not effectively welcome the class with any positive intent (I'm not talking about being 'gung-ho' either, or 'overly ebullient' – students get weary of that quickly . . .), whose teaching 'style' and communication 'style' is boring, unengaging and lacking in any enthusiasm, whose approach and manner do not command the basic respect of children, who give little positive feedback and encourage, and whose discipline 'style' is 'naggy', nit-picking and frequently negative. I've seen classes who will patiently put up with such teaching for a day – most classes won't.

Our 'claim' to authority is earned within the effectiveness of our teaching and management, and that kind of authority needs both goodwill *and* skill. (See Chapters 4 and 5).

Developing assertive skills

Non-assertive behaviour

Non-assertive behaviours in teachers arise in part from temperament and in part from a strong need to 'be liked' by the students. I have known teachers whose need for 'approval' and 'liking' (in their students) consequently sees them as frustrated, at times 'pleading' in their leadership role: 'Come on guys, please – come on please be quiet everyone.' 'Boys, you know you should be doing that don't you?' This teacher, whether to the whole class or the individuals, *sounds* as if he didn't believe he would be taken seriously. The use of questions ('Why are you being so noisy, guys?') or 'weak' directions ('*Please be* quiet, guys – come on', 'I'd *really* like you to be quiet now, guys') quickly see the class degenerate into a form of lateral tyranny. Students often come in late to class and ignore him (en route to seats), call out frequently, speak very noisily, tell him his work is 'boooring!'

While this teacher had goodwill he found it hard to speak out confidently and assert his fundamental right to address inappropriate and disruptive behaviours. Such teachers, in some schools, may experience patterns of fractious and disruptive behaviours even in 'reasonable' students. While they believe they *sound* 'pleasant and reasonable', they 'come across' as 'apologetic' and overly deferent: 'I'm nice to them why can't they be nice to me?' While their demeanour and body language (in their minds) seeks to show they care (they do) it may well be interpreted as 'weakness' by the students. This is unfortunate.

Non-assertive behaviour may also be the result of lack of conscious skill – not knowing what to do, *or say* , when under pressure from challenging student behaviours.

Assertive behaviour in teachers

Assertion is often confused with concepts like 'bossiness', 'controlling', 'forcing' others; of being 'pushy' in order to 'win'. For some teachers their discomfort with developing appropriate (at times very necessary) assertive leadership arises from confusion about what reasonably constitutes assertive behaviour.

Being 'pushy', 'bossy', 'sharp', 'authoritarian' will sometimes get a sense of immediate 'control' and compliance in some students in some schools. In other schools such teacher behaviour will be derided by students and form the basis for peer entertainment. Such behaviour will also quickly affect the working relationships teachers (even supply teachers) need to build with their students. Being assertive is not about 'one's' power, as 'my' power, it is concerned with using one's power 'for' and 'with' the student – using our 'adultness' to address the situation and behaviour with some conscious focus, expectation and clarity.

Assertion involves stating one's needs, wants and expectations 'clearly', 'firmly', 'assuredly' and respectfully (that's the hard bit – respectfully). Some teachers find it hard to hold concepts like 'asserting' and 'respecting' together. It is possible, in fact it is essential, as a teacher-leader.

Being assertive is also about not merely letting the student(s) take the initiative for 'how things will be', or how we (as teachers) are treated. I find it disconcerting, at times distressing, when I see older students treating a teacher 'like dirt'; being verbally rude, dismissive, ignoring – treating them as if they have no visible leadership role or presence.

Being assertive is in part being consciously focused (and skilled) in communicating our rights but also being secure in our self as a person, as a professional. Our self-worth, as a teacher, is not tied to our students' 'approval'. The way we gain acceptance, acknowledgement, affirmation and even 'approval' is through the quality and nature of the leadership we *characteristically* exercise.

When children swear at us (as some will in some schools on some days, 'the little b ——-s!' – just joking) their swearing – of itself – cannot hurt our self-esteem. While I do not like it when children swear at me and I will always address it, I am not actually hurt by it; I see their outburst at me as their 'problem behaviour'. That doesn't mean I excuse the swearing behaviour – particularly swearing directed *at* me (as distinct from frustration swearing). It does mean I need to professionally address this behaviour with appropriate assertion. 'Michael, I don't ever swear at you, I don't expect you to swear at me.' Our tone and manner need to be consistent with the assertion we need (or want) to exercise.

If the child's swearing is *sotto voce* (in passing, as it were, as he walks away from us) then a quieter, 'one-to-one' approach is more appropriate. Direct the child aside, in class: 'Sean, I don't use language like that with you . . . if you're uptight with me you need to find another way of telling me, OK? Now let's look at your work.'

If the child is swearing out of confused anger and distress, directly *at* me, I find it helpful to express the assertive behaviour calmly, clearly and specifically: 'I can see you are really upset, Melissa. 'Come with me now; you can have some calming-down (or 'cool-off time') and we can sort it out later.' Most students will, then, take some time-out. (Often with necessary senior teacher support; p. 90). Just angrily telling the student she *shouldn't* swear (when in a temper) or asking if 'that's the kind of language she uses at home' will only increase the current arousal and create unworkable conflict.

Basic skills of assertion

When communicating assertively we are emphasizing how our rights, or others' rights, are affected by the disruptive *behaviours* of those we need to discipline.

Case example

First day with a challenging Year 10 class. The female supply teacher arrives for her first session with these students. Early in the lesson a male student exercises his pathetic brand of humour: 'Ay, Miss – you look like you'd do a good bit part in *Pretty Woman*, eh?' At this he looks around to pick up some collusive peer laughter. She pauses, the laughter dies down. She looks directly at him moves a few feet closer to him (not too close) and says: 'I don't make comments about your body or clothing. I don't expect you to make comments about mine.' The class (and the student) sense the teacher is serious, sure, firm, but not 'fazed'. The student blusters out 'Gees – I was only joking!' The teacher – in a calm, assertive voice – says: 'I don't see it as a joke. I don't expect those kinds of jokes in our class.' (By using inclusive language 'our' she includes a small, but crucial, note of *shared* expectation.)

She drops eye-contact, walks back to the front of the room, scans the whole-class group and says: 'Right, everyone, show's over, let's get back to what we are here for.' If you were an observer that day you would have *sensed* (palpably) this teacher's confidence in herself to address this 'cocksparrow' behaviour. Caveat: if the student continues with such behaviour it will be wise to use the supported time-out option (p. 90). The least effective teacher behaviour in such instances is to argue, shout or plead or 'reason'.

- Use stable, direct eye-contact. Not too close!
- It can help, on occasion, to count to three before saying what you want/need to say.
- 'Open body language' – avoid pointing, jabbing, gesticulating fingers. An open hand, palm outwards, to make a point. While this might sound like 'minutiae', it is important to have some congruence between confident assertive body language and what we say.
- Do not enter into an argument with the student. Keep what you want (and need) to say brief and address the issue or behaviour (avoid verbally 'attacking' the student – though we are sorely tempted to at times).
- If our assertion focuses on a rule, we do not need to defend the rule (or right), just fairly assert the rule or (with older, secondary, students reassert the right affected).
- Brief, clear, 'I' statements carry the intended assertion in terms of what you *do not*, or *do*, want to occur:

    'I don't speak to you rudely, I don't expect you to speak rudely to me.' Young children may be confused by the qualifier 'rudely' (re their 'tone' or 'manner'). It will often help when addressing 'rudeness' in infants to clarify first by *briefly* describing their behaviour then assert, 'Sean, your voice sounds nasty (or mean, or not kind or loud and bad-tempered or like you don't care). I don't like that. I want you to use a kinder voice. Thanks'.

    'You're pointing your finger and shouting at me . . . I don't like that. If you want to speak to me use a nicer voice.'

    'Think about how your voice sounds.'

    When we assert like this it doesn't change the *fact* that the student has been rude, arrogant or abusive. It does ratify (in public hearing of other students) what we believe is unacceptable about the student's *behaviour*. We should always address the behaviour not attack the person. We have made our point, *clearly*, firmly and as unambiguously as we can.

- Regarding assertive *language*, it may sound a bit 'twee', a bit 'mechanical', to have some stock phrases in one's repertoire. However, when we're under pressure to say and do something – in the emotional moment – the last thing we'll be thinking of is *what* to say. When we are frustrated or angry with a student's behaviour 'appropriate' words do not come easily. Having some core assertive phrases will support a *less* stressful behaviour at the moment we need to assert; we'll feel more secure in having thought through some of the likely scenarios. As a mentor I encourage some 'personal practice' (even in front of a mirror). Corny as it might sound, these assertive skills are *skills*: they benefit from some 'practice' to increase the 'comfort zone' in one's behaviour management and leadership.

- Avoid using unhelpful questions when addressing disruptive behaviour (p. 46ff); when we assert we do not want to discuss the merits of relative aspects of disruptive student behaviours. I have seen teachers trying to make their discipline 'point' by saying things like:

  '*Would you mind* facing this way, please?'

  '*Can you not call* out, please?'

  'Please don't be rude to me', or 'Why are you being rude to me?'

  It will be much more appropriate to assert to the student that he *is* being rude (in a particular way) and direct him to stop/remember 'our rule for . . . ' Even in our basic day-to-day discipline an appropriate *assertive tone* will carry intent to the language we use. Instead of the 'reasonable' and 'nice' questioning ('*Would you . . . ?*', '*Can you . . . ?*'), a firm, confident, description and direction will more convincingly carry our intent and expectation: 'Some students are working too noisily. Bring the noise down to quiet working talk. Thanks.' (See p. 43).

- Having assertively made our point, it will help to bring any emotional arousal 'down', as it were. It may be appropriate to direct the student to cool-off time or even an exit from the room time-out. Some students will often 'sulk' or 'get angry' because we said 'stuff' to them in a firm voice (as in the example noted on p. 32).

- Always make the effort, later that day, to repair and rebuild with the student. This is an easily missed aspect of our overall management. While we may find it difficult to *want* to make the effort to repair and rebuild it is necessary, it demonstrates we care, that there are no hard feelings (at least on our part).

Sometimes repairing and rebuilding necessitate some mediating between students who were (earlier) in conflict in the classroom. On such occasions it might be difficult to carry through the necessary 'mediation' if you are a 'day-cover' supply teacher. In the short-term, when the conflict occurs in the classroom, it will be enough to exercise appropriate time-out options, then later have at least a brief word with the two students before the day's end. It can help to leave a thoughtfully worded note (alongside the due incident report sheet) that you have spoken to the students concerned (one to one) about the issue and that you would have liked to have had time for a further mediation session but this was not possible (as you are a day-cover teacher). You can at least demonstrate that degree of professionalism without actually telling your colleagues they should set up some mediation.

Assertion in discipline

When we are assertive in our discipline we are using our appropriate adult power to affirm core rights, clarify expectations and bring some protection to people's rights and feelings. When we hear a student, humourously, nastily or sometimes viciously put another student down in class (or in the playground), our assertive behaviour (what we say; how we say it; what we decide to do) addresses the injustice of the abuse while communicating our feeling about the abuse.

I sometimes hear students trading homophobic slurs in the classrooms I teach in. I never ignore or make light of such language, even if If the put-down is a 'quiet aside' between students.

I also sometimes hear older students in some schools using friendly banter in the classroom: 'bitch', 'dropkick', 'a__hole', 'd__head', 'poofter', 'wanker' ('Give us that pen, you d__head.'). When I address such behaviour students will often say they are 'just mucking around', 'It's no big deal, she doesn't care if I call her bitch, she's my friend'. My response is invariably: 'I *care* how *we* speak in *our* classroom. We've got a rule for respect that includes the way we speak to one another. I want you to care too.'

In such cases the assertion is 'quiet', one to one; but (again) we will brook no discussion (in the heat of the moment). Where the student's put-down has a nastier tone: 'That's a put-down. I don't *ever* expect that language in *our* classroom/school'. The perpetrator will often say 'It was just a joke!! Get real – can't you even take a joke?' An equally firm reframing is also part of our assertive response: 'In our class that is not a joke and it stops now.' At this point it is important that teacher does not brook further discussion, but de-escalates the residual tension.

The whole class has been witness to this piece of 'fanfare' so it is important to point out to them that 'The show's over – let's get back to what we're here for'. The perpetrator often sits sulking at this point (we have ruined their little 'game').

If the student becomes really nasty, and repeatedly abusive (following such teacher discipline), it will be necessary to direct them to formal time-out (p. 89). The difficult, but necessary, step will be to then occasion some repairing and rebuilding with the student *later* in the day (p. 79ff). Such 'repairing and rebuilding' may also necessitate some mediation between perpetrator and victim (a process that will need the support of a senior colleague).

Accents, dialects and language

I have been working in the UK for many years now and have become used to the variety of accents across the United 'Queendom'. I have also noticed that accents, dialect and manner of speech can have an effect on classroom behaviour.

Teachers for whom English is not their first language will sometimes experience teasing laughter from children (particularly older children) 'What did ya say, Sir?!' 'We can't understand ya.' It will help to discuss with colleagues how they might thoughtfully address this issue should it arise. It will help, for example, to plan ahead what you might say to the class group: 'You will have already noticed my accent is different from what you may be used to. I might *mis*-pronounce words from time to time. I work hard on my English and I thank you all, already, for your understanding support.' If such an explanation is given *confidently*, positively, tactfully and with good humour, students are normally thankful 'the issue' is out in the open' and their residual goodwill is invited (Rogers, 2000a. pp. 83–4).

One's diction, clarity, pronunciation and rate of speech are all important aspects of our professional teaching. The ability to speak and communicate clearly are crucial to effective teaching. Slowing one's speech and enunciating more clearly will help; *not* too slow, or *too* exaggerated. (I've even had to ask some Scottish and Welsh colleagues to do that for me; they have the advantage of watching *Neighbours*, I've watched *Taggart* but I still struggle with some Scottish accents – no offence!)

When speaking to a group of students it is also important visually to scan the group, make transitional eye-contact and make a conscious effort not to mumble or drop one's head or voice. (Too soft, too loud?) It can help to ask a trusted colleague for some professional feedback on this if you have genuine concerns.

Dress and culture

If you choose to wear cultural attire (as part of your daily dress) it will be important to recognize that in some schools such attire may see students overly intrigued and overly focusing on a teacher's dress/headwear/jewellery, etc. (Why wouldn't they?) This is natural and should not be the cause of defensiveness in the teacher. Again, a brief explanation is normally enough if the students show overt, or distracting, curiosity.

For some teachers, teaching in Britain for the first time may prove a challenge. If their first language is not English the cultural and social mores of some children may appear 'brash', 'insensitive', 'rude', even 'arrogant'. These behaviours are, of course, universal among *school children*; however, in non-Western cultures the behaviour I have noted and described may not normally be present in schools.

While such behaviour is not to be condoned by teachers it is important to be professionally aware that many children today do not easily, quickly or *simply* acquiesce to a teacher's authority simply *because* they are a teacher. Some teachers may simply assume that children *should* – and *must* – obey their teachers because they have the *title* or *role* of teacher. These days, more than ever, teachers have to 'earn' their leadership 'status' through their ability to engage with and relate to children; to teach with confidence, enthusiasm and skill and be able to exercise appropriate discipline in as positive a way as possible. Above all they need to demonstrate that they respect their students, that they care about them, their learning and their well-being (even if they are only teaching for a single day).

There are some social and cultural mores, attitudes and behaviours that we need to be aware of beyond our own familiar cultural environment. It is hoped that the skills and approaches in this book will enable you to heighten your cross-cultural awareness as a teacher.

4

A daily discipline plan: key discipline and management skills

The tongue
is where
the mind
comes out
into the open

Lips move
so to speak

The tongue
is where
the mind
comes out
into the open

Mind
what you say.
(Steve Turner)

A discipline plan can assist overall confidence in our role as supply teacher. Moving transitionally between different kinds of schools will bring us in contact with a range of 'discipline policies', 'practices' and 'systems'. The following discipline plan and the key skills have a wide, generative, utility.

A 'discipline plan' is a fundamental framework for our discipline leadership. Its emphasis lies in having thought through likely scenarios in which we need to exercise discipline and planning thoughtful and (potentially) more effective ways to address the typical range of disruptive behaviours that we may have to face. While we will need to plan for typical lessons we have to teach, we also need to plan for what we can do and say in discipline settings when students call out, 'talk while the teacher is talking', push/shove, speak loudly in class learning time, 'wander', use inappropriate or swearing language or become hostile or even aggressive (behaviour we hope we won't have to face too often).

The key features of such a plan are:

- The *re*framing of rules and routines for the day(s) of teaching while *you* are the teacher-leader.
- A framework of *least-to-most* discipline 'interventions' with special reference to the 'language of discipline'.
- A conscious awareness of *assertive* language where appropriate (see also Chapter 3).
- When, and how, to use time-out options.
- Thoughtful use of follow-up/follow-through procedures.

Least to most intrusive discipline

Some teachers have an overly intrusive language of correction expressed in negative language ('don't . . .', 'can't . . .', 'shouldn't . . .', 'give me that now!' – this to a student who has a pack of Pokemon cards on his desk and is fiddling with them instead of working). One hardly needs to be highly 'intrusive' over issues like lateness, calling out or distracting *objets d'art*. When we *pace* the degree of corrective intrusiveness we also place relative moral weight on *what* behaviours we address and *how* we address them.

The Pokemon cards (for example) can be dealt with by a 'directed choice': 'Patrick, nice cards; I want you to put them in your locker-tray or on my table. Thanks.' The teacher will not argue about *whether* the student was actually playing with them ('Don't lie to me!') but will refocus the student to the directed choice and to the required work and then give him some 'take-up time' (p. 43) thus keeping a small incident 'least intrusive'.

Language skills

This chapter addresses the crucial nature of language in our discipline. The utility and intent in our language and its ability to engage some co-operation in our students is dependent on our self-confidence, tone of voice, *relaxed* vigilance and our intentional respect *within* the vehicle of language. Our discipline language is never an end in itself (cessation of distracting and disruptive behaviour); it is the means of effecting a positive working relationship between the teacher and the individual, the teacher and the group.

Tactical ignoring

Throughout this book I've used the term *tactical* ignoring. When students are chatting while the teacher is trying to address the whole class, when students are loudly fiddling with pens (or other distracting items), when students call out or walk in late (without a brief apology or at least an acknowledgement of the teacher) these are behaviours that should not be ignored (even *tactically*). These behaviours need positive teacher management (a key theme in this book). We should never 'ignore' verbal hostility (even rudeness) or *any* aggressive behaviours (verbal or physical).

There are, however, some aspects of a student's behaviour we can skilfully, consciously, decisively and *tactically* ignore. When a student 'pouts', 'rolls their eyes', 'sighs' because we have directed them to so something really difficult like, 'remember the hands-up rule – thanks', we do not need to 'feed' their non-verbal 'attitude' by saying things like 'Don't sigh at me – I've got a degree, I'm a teacher!'

Learning when, and in what contexts, to tactically ignore

Tactical ignoring is a context-dependent skill. It has its most judicious use when seeking to keep the focus of our discipline on the 'primary' issues we are seeking to address and not over-servicing 'secondary' behaviours (Rogers, 2000a).

If you ask a student, for example, to put his chewing gum in the bin (even though '*all* the "normal" teachers *always* allow students to chew gum here') it may go something like this:

Teacher	Sees the student viscously engaged in chewing and approaches: 'Craig, how's the work going?' (She has a brief, task-focused chat.) As she moves off she says: 'The bin's over there.'
Student	'Eh?'
Teacher	'The bin's over there' (the teacher non-verbally cues to her own mouth to heighten the 'cognitive shortfall' re the incidental direction about the gum).
Student	'Gees! Other teachers don't care if we chew gum.' The student has a whining tone to his voice. This 'secondary' behaviour is sometimes more annoying than the 'primary' issue.
Teacher	The teacher, here, *tactically* ignores the whining tone, the leaning back posture, the 'tut-tutting'. She partially agrees with the student but keeps the focus on the primary issue (the fair rule about chewing gum). 'Maybe your regular teacher does (partial agreement); the school rule is clear though. The bin is over there. Thanks.' At this point the teacher walks away (giving the student some take-up time). The teacher continues to walk around the room helping, encouraging, refocusing and giving feedback. By giving some take-up time the teacher makes it easier for the student to co-operate; she doesn't 'stand over him' as it were.

The student slopes off to the bin, muttering ('this class is a repressive regime'). He spits the chewing gum in the bin and slopes off back to his seat, slumps in and slowly ('oh so slowly') starts getting some work done. All this behaviour is 'secondary' to the main issue of gum-in-bin and is *tactically* ignored by the supply teacher.

Imagine if she were to go over to the lad (en route to/from the bin) and say 'Look! Don't you make *such a fuss* about a little thing like chewing gum. When you put gum in the bin you do it quietly – alright?'

If the student chooses not to put the gum in the bin (despite 'take-up time') the teacher knows the issue is not the gum or the fair rule – it is an incipient power struggle. In such a case she will (later) give the student a deferred consequence (p. 86ff).

In this typical behaviour episode *tactical* ignoring is a significant feature of the teacher's overall 'discipline'; it has enabled her to be both *relaxedly* vigilant and positive.

Giving directions in discipline situations

The most common language we tend to use in a discipline context is the teacher's direction. Where possible it will help co-operation in our students if we use directions that are:

- *positive in intent and form*. Rather than say *'Don't* call out in class' or *'Don't* talk while I'm teaching' or *'Don't* lean back in your seat' try positive forms such as 'Hands up (without calling out) thanks'. If we need to qualify with a 'negative caveat' keep the positive intention (as above) in the direction. 'Craig (. . .) Four on the floor with your seat', 'Eyes and ears this way thanks – without talking' rather than simply 'Don't talk while I'm teaching';
- when addressing individual students, *always use their first name*. If it isn't known, ask;
- *behavioural*. focus on the behaviour you want and expect (and that is appropriate within the rules), for example, *'looking this way* and *listening* thanks'. This to a couple of students 'gas-bagging' while the teacher is engaged in whole-class teaching. If the students 'answer back' ('Other students were talking too!') it will be enough to 'block' and redirect (see later p. 50ff);
- *brief*; brevity is important. The purpose of corrective discipline is to address the thoughtless, distracting or disruptive behaviour and refocus back to the *core business of teaching and learning*. That is why it is important not to start discussions, 'debates' or arguments about 'who did or didn't do what they should or shouldn't be doing' or whether 'teachers allow us to have chewing gum' (or whatever);
- *allow some take-up time* (where appropriate). When we give a direction it can often help to give the student some take-up time (Rogers, 2000a) Take-up-time refers to the teacher consciously giving the direction or reminder, and removing eye-contact and spatial proximity to consciously convey expectation and minimize unnecessary confrontation (see later). Another form of take-up time occurs when we use tactical pausing (. . .) in direction or reminders.

Incidental direction

With older students (upper primary/secondary) discipline directions can often be given 'incidentally' by drawing the student's attention to what it is they are doing that is forgetful, distracting or disruptive. On such occasions it may well be enough to encourage or remind by 'describing the obvious' (Rogers, 2000a). Several students come into class with their hats on. The teacher simply taps her own head as she says 'Sean (. . .) Adam, (. . .) Bilal (. . .) your hats'. A student is fiddling with a skateboard while the teacher is explaining a teaching point to the class group. She tactically pauses in what she was saying (. . .) 'Excuse me, Craig isn't it?' 'Yeah.' (He stops fiddling with the object.) She looks briefly at the skateboard (without moving towards Craig) and adds: 'It's distracting – the skateboard I mean.' She adds a brief 'Thanks' to (already) convey expectation. She turns her eyes away and resumes the flow of the lesson giving the student take-up time. There is an 'as-if-ness' to the tone of her voice. If Craig continues fiddling she will give a directed choice (e.g. 'I want you to put that toy in your pencil case, or I can put it on the table up here until recess'). What she won't do is make this small issue into a major one by simply ordering the student to give her the distracting toy or snatching it up.

Sometimes we'll need to add a direction to the descriptive comment, e.g.: 'Melissa and Paula (. . .) you're talking while I'm teaching our class (. . .) (the descriptive comment). 'Looking this way and *listening*. Thanks' (the behavioural direction part).

Not all behaviour is *intentionally* disruptive. It may well be 'forgetful' behaviour or thoughtlessly distracting as when a student is fiddling with his pencil case, or tapping idly with a pen or leaning back a little too motorically; behaviours which are distracting when the teacher is engaged in whole-class teaching. By using incidental language we keep the corrective flow more invitational and potentially co-operative.

Directions with infants

When giving directions to infants we particularly need to be clear, direct, behaviourally focused and appropriately brief. 'Cross your legs (teacher looks at three or four students) like that . . . and looking this way and listening.' 'This is not talking time, it is listening time. Everybody (teacher scans the group) needs to be . . . ' (teacher then specifically directs to appropriate 'on the carpet time' behaviour).

With infants it can help to have a simple, large, colourful poster illustrating 'on the carpet' behaviour during group discussion/teaching time: these posters (will) illustrate students sitting ('cross-legged'), facing the front and a few hands-up (without calling out).

Rule reminders

Basic as it sounds, the most common form of 'discipline language' is the rule reminder/question. If the rules are clear and fair, it is often enough to remind the individual (or group) by referring directly (and briefly) to that rule: 'Jason (. . .) we've got a rule for asking questions.' This to a student (grade 4) calling out during whole-class discussion. In this case the teacher is using the *rule reminder* (reference to the rule) as a descriptive reminder, e.g. 'Paula (. . .), Hannah (. . .) remember our rule for working talk. Thanks.' This is said (quietly) to two students working too loudly during on-task learning time.

If several (or more) students are calling out during instructional time the rule reminder will be given to the whole class after a brief, descriptive, preface. As the teacher visually scans the class she holds up a 'blocking hand', stops talking herself, *tactically* pauses (. . .) – as if to say 'stop and listen'. She then says, 'A number of students are calling out without (and with) their hands up' (the descriptive preface). 'Remember our class rule for questions and class discussion. Thanks' (the rule reminder).

If the rules have been clarified *initially*, it will not be necessary to qualify the reminder: e.g. ' . . . hands up without calling out, and one at a time'. Those elements will have been discussed and even published on a rule-poster. Often, when giving a rule reminder, the teacher will physically cue back to the rule-poster.

It can also be helpful to use rule questions, in 'one-to-one' settings during on-task learning time, e.g. 'Michelle and Amy what's *our* rule about safe use of equipment?' (this to two infants being a little too silly with paint brushes).

When giving rule reminders/questions it can help to use inclusive language: 'our', 'us', 'we', 'all of us here', 'everyone', 'together'.

Questions in a discipline situation

The most common, and least helpful, question in a discipline context is the interrogative 'Why?' e.g. '*Why* are you calling out?' '*Why* are you talking when I'm trying to explain something to the class?'

A similarly unhelpful form is 'are you?' e.g. '*Are you* talking?' (this from a teacher 'disciplining' a couple of students talking while the teacher is engaged in whole-class teaching). Some teachers will frequently 'tack' interrogatives to the end of a discipline statement: 'You're not supposed to be doing that now *are you*?' The other commonly unhelpful use of a question is to cue it as if it was a direction: 'Would you give that to me now?' (this to a student fiddling – annoyingly – with a distracting object while the teacher is engaged in whole-class teaching).

Do we really want to know '*why*' a student is calling out, fiddling with a skateboard, leaning back in their seat, talking while the teacher is talking, or rolling on the carpet (hopefully only at infant level!)?

If our tone is 'snappy' or 'bossy' the interrogative form can lead to very counter-productive management. The supply teacher notices one of his grade 6 students is not working during on-task learning time. He walks over to him and asks him '*why*' he hasn't started (like the other students). 'I don't have a pen.' The student's reply is a bit too sulky for this teacher; the student's tone triggers a louder, more insistent interrogative from the teacher:

Teacher	'Other students have got pens, *why* haven't you got a pen?'
Student	'Gees! (the student sounds rattled, but senses he can 'work' this new, supply teacher); people don't bring pens sometimes you know – I just forgot, all right?' The student's flippant, sarcastic tone – leaning back in his seat – is really annoying the teacher.
Teacher	'Look – don't you speak to me like that!'
Student	'Like what! Gees – you're hassling me about a pen!'
Teacher	'I'm not hassling you – *is it so hard* to bring a pen to class?' (another unhelpful question at *this* point in the lesson, particularly as the student is contestably aware of his peers watching

	him play out some 'attentional- power' with the 'new' teacher).
Teacher	'Right! Just get a pen from one of your friends (if you've got any).' He mutters this a little too loud; the sarcasm obviously doesn't help.
Student	The student pushes back his seat (dramatically?) and says, 'Alright I'll get a pen if you really want.' He says this in a sing-song staccato voice replete with sigh and rolled eyes. His classmate says he's not going to lend him a pen: 'I didn't get the last one back!' The student walks back to the teacher (many in the class are enjoying this 'entertainment', it's better than maths!). 'He won't give me a pen!' The student, here, effects a whine, a slack mouth, hunched shoulders.
Teacher	The teacher has had enough of this little so-and-so! 'Right get out, go on – *get out*! You can go to the principal for all I care.'
Student	'Yeah, well I'm going.' He mutters loudly, 'It's a shit class anyway!' Of course, when the student arrives at the principal's office and is asked what he is there for the student merely says 'I didn't have a pen.' Most students omit the chain of reactive events that saw the teacher interpret this 'small incident' (no pen) as a need in the teacher to 'win' ('I *must* prove I'm in control here!' 'No student should speak to a teacher like that. Students *should* respect their teachers!'

The reality, of course, is somewhat different. Gaining respect from a student is never a fait accompli; it doesn't simply accrue to our role. We earn respect by the kind of leadership we exercise. Further if we *characteristically* explain such events (as the above) as role demands ('children *must* respect their teachers', '*must* do what the teacher says, *without* answering back') we will be more stressed than we need to be. The reality in teaching is that there will be students who answer back, whose body language, tone, demeanour and manner is flippant, rude even arrogant. While we clearly have to address such behaviours, characteristically *demanding* beliefs will actually increase our stress level and reduce our effective coping abilities.

This is *not* a contrived situation. while we can understand that some of these 'cock-sparrows' can really be annoying, as the teacher-leader we need to:

- avoid pointless interrogatives *in discipline* situations (use descriptive or directive, or rule-reminding forms of discipline language);
- keep the focus on the 'primary' issue – the need to 'face the front and listen', to get a pen, and start 'work'. Avoid focusing on the 'secondary behaviours': the student's casual, indifferent body language, the whining or whingeing tone of voice, the rolled eyes, the sibilant sigh.

In this case it would have been basic prevention for the supply teacher to bring a box of spare pens, pencil, ruler, paper, etc. (p. 7).

If the student refuses to work or co-operate, decide whether to use an immediate or deferred consequence (p. 86ff).

Direct imperative questions

For behaviour that is distracting, disruptive (but not hostile or aggressive) the use of direct questions is often appropriate. A direct question – asked in a positive (non-accusatory) tone by the teacher – focuses on the student's responsibility in the discipline situation being addressed. A direct imperative question focuses on calling the student to their responsibility, e.g. 'What . . . ?', 'Where . . . ?', 'When . . . ?', 'How . . . ?' For example, '*What* are you doing?', '*What's* happening here?', '*What's* our rule for? (be specific)', '*Where* should you be working now?', '*How* will you complete this piece of work?', '*When* do you think you need to have it finished?'

When students are asked the general questions 'What are you doing?' (with respect to disruptive behaviour) they will often say 'Nothing' in reply. A brief description of what they were doing that was distracting or disruptive helps refocus their responsibility prior to the second question:'What should you be doing so that others can get on with their work?' 'What could you do so that . . .?'

This second question, '*What* should you be doing now?', 'What is our rule for . . . ?' is asking the student to make the value judgement and commit themselves to the appropriate and fair behaviour. If the student doesn't 'know' what they need to do that is appropriate, or chooses to play the attention-power 'game', 'I don't know, you tell me', direct them to what they should be doing, or it will be enough to make the consequences clear.

This 'form' of 'discipline dialogue' is appropriate for older children (middle, upper primary). Although some infants, too, will often respond 'constructively' to this form of 'dialogue'.

As with all discipline our leadership focus is on supporting the child to see that it is his behaviour that is unacceptable (even if it is 'attention-ally' fun). It is unnecessary to 'judge' or 'criticize' the child. It is the student's *behaviour* that affects the rights of others around them: the right to learn, to respect, to safety, to teach. If our concern for the child's welfare and teaching is paramount, the use of such questions becomes a 'means to an end'. The aim of our discipline is to promote responsibility for one's behaviour and respect for mutual rights.

Blocking, partial agreement and redirecting

Blocking and *redirection* are ways of keeping one's discipline focused on the 'primary' issue in a discipline transaction. A student is calling out in whole-class instruction time. The teacher gives a brief rule reminder (wanting, then, to focus on students who are not calling out, who *are* attending and who are putting their hands up to ask questions or make a point). 'Michael (. . .) remember our class rule for asking questions.' Michael responds with 'But, Miss; other students call out'. The teacher makes a small blocking gesture (palm out/upward) and repeats the rule reminder (redirecting) as she scans the sea of faces and targets the students with their hand up and who are not calling out: 'Yes, Sean, Patrick, Tran . . . 1, 2, 3 . . . Sean, what's your question?' The blocking gesture and words make it clear the teacher will not engage in excuses or avoidance behaviours.

Partial agreement refers to the acknowledgement we give – as teachers – to what the student is saying but redirects to the important issue 'at the moment' (as it were). One of the more common behaviours faced by supply teachers is when students compare what their regular teacher allows with what the supply teacher won't allow. In these cases partial agreement says 'Maybe Ms X (or Mr Y) allows you to . . . The school rule (however) is . . . '. If there is no school rule, or routine, or normative expectation as such, we can say 'Maybe Ms X says it's OK; today we will be doing . . . ' or 'I expect you to . . . ' If the student argues again, we can make the consequences of their refusal to co-operate clear. The important thing when 'partially agreeing' (as in all discipline) is not to sound smug or confrontational.

On many occasions – in high schools – I have addressed secreted Walkman users and even mobile phone users in this way. I had a Year 10 student once say (on receipt of a rule reminder about using Walkmans in class time) that 'she' – he pointed to a young newly qualified teacher (NQT) I was mentoring – 'She don't care if I have it on – long as I get my work done'. His tone wasn't nasty, he was (I'm sure) telling the truth. Rather than suggest I was more managerially competent ('I don't care what she does, I've been teaching for 117 years and I'm telling you to give me that Walkman!') this is an occasion when *partial agreement* and redirection is appropriate.

Teacher	'Maybe Ms Snooks doesn't mind you playing your Walkman (the partial agreement). What's the school rule, Basil?' (the direct question quickly focuses on the rule and his responsibility).
Student	'I told you, long as I get my work done . . . '
Teacher	'You told me (the partial agreement); what's the school rule?' (the redirection).
Student	'Gees.'
Teacher	'I'm sure you know the fair rule, Basil' (belief in the student's comprehension/co-operation). 'I'll come and check your work later – see how you're going.' By walking away (at this point) we give some take-up time, some basic trust and a task reminder.

If the student had refused to take the Walkman ear-buds out we can give a directed choice ('In your bag or on my table') or a deferred consequence ('If you choose not to put it away, I'll need to follow this up with you at recess'). Either way we avoid arguing or snatching the expensive, distracting, item. We leave the responsibility *with* the student.

Commands

There are times when it is necessary, even essential, to command students. Any hostile or aggressive behaviours in/out of class will require a firm, decisive, even sharp, tone of voice to immediately gain attention, 'Troy, Craig (. . .) move away now.' After the *initial* raised, 'sharp' voice it will help to 'drop' the voice tone to a firm, steady, clear assertive direction or command. If we *keep* the whole of the direction, assertion or command at an overly raised voice, we increase and extend too much emotional arousal. It is important to use a decisive, unambiguously commanding voice tone, rather than an aggressive tone of voice. 'Move away from each other now. Troy over there (...) Craig over there (...) *now.*'

It is important also not to waste energy, effort or time trying to address secondary issues such as a student's protestations about 'who started it', or their discounting 'Other kids did stuff too!' Command the student; repeat if necessary and 'calm' the rest of the audience. 'All right everyone (scan the group) the show's over ... back to work.'

Humour

We need to be careful when using humour with a new group, not knowing the individuals and their idiosyncratic temperaments it is easy to miscue with humour; where we intended to lighten, a student may infer a put-down.

Most humour, in the early meeting with a class, will be relaxed, natural humour arising out of an incident, event, words we use, even some aspect of our teaching. When we 'run' with such natural humour and shared laughter we show our basic shared humanity. Irony, a pun, a 'spoonerism', can all lighten the shared day (or 'shighten the lared day').

- Avoid *any* sarcasm; students will easily hear our intent even if we don't use sarcastic language.
- Use humour to defuse tense situations or reframe by using repartee or bon mot.

On the way into class recently, one of the students passed some rather loud, and foul, flatulence. Another student remarked, loudly, quickly 'Jesus Christ'. I added quickly, 'Is He a student here as well?'

'What?'

'Jesus – is He a student here as well?' I was trying to get the student to briefly – transitionally – think about what he'd said. He twigged, 'Nah'. I smiled back, eyes raised to indicate we both knew.

To the lad who had passed that foul 'something' on to the ether I *whispered*, 'We normally bury dead animals before we come into class'. He grinned, and took his seat. A tense moment was reframed but I wish I'd had some air freshener as well!

Discipline language/discipline plan

In stressing the importance of discipline (guiding/corrective) *language*, I want to stress – yet again – that mere words are not enough to create a positive, confident, relational, form of communication.

While language – even the *actual* words – are very important, what carries the confidence, and positive intent is our *characteristic* tone of voice, use of eye-contact, relational proximity, our expectancy and our confidence (or our uncertainty).

While this sounds like minutiae, *taken together* it presents our overall leadership behaviour:

- Is our *characteristic* tone of voice confident, positive, anxious, querulous, pleading?
- Does our *characteristic* body language look confident, expectant of co-operation, or does it look tense or uncertain?
- When we come into a student's personal space are we aware of the 'invitational presence'? Do we merely pick up a student's work without asking? Are we aware of entering their 'personal space' considerately? It's basic emotional intelligence.

Key questions to be addressed in one's overall management plan

As noted many times in this text, colleague support is a crucial feature of a workable, even a successful, teaching day. In most schools supply teachers will receive a 'supply teacher kit' (see Chapter 2) – a checklist cum framework for a normative teaching day. This 'kit' will address the basic (but essential)routines that can support the smooth running of a teaching day for supply teacher and students alike. Many schools will have a supply teacher support policy. A key feature of such a 'policy' is a nominated colleague who acts as a 'teaching buddy' for the day – a colleague with allocated responsibility who can act as a collegial reference for questions, clarifications and moral support. They will normally meet at the outset of the day and at lunch recess for a chat and are often the first port of call for exit/time-out procedures. The classroom assistant/ teaching assistant (if one is allocated to your class) can also be an invaluable source of 'in-house' assistance and support.

In less supportive schools there may well be minimal moral support and minimal contextual information to professionally support the day's teaching. In such schools it can help to proactively ask the questions you need answers to in order more effectively to cope, and teach, that day. If you don't ask, in some schools it may be assumed that you know.

Some years ago I conducted research on colleague support in schools (Rogers, 1999) and in a number of secondary schools I asked questions such as 'In what ways does the school *consciously* support supply teachers?' That question alone saw many senior staff scratching their heads. Beyond the handing over of a student attendance roll and *maybe*, a map and a quick visit to the staffroom, they were effectively *on their own* for the rest of the teaching day.

While it may well be argued that a professional teacher should know how to work with any class, that's not the primary issue. When a new teacher, first time in a school, does not know the idiosyncratic culture, norms and especially *daily* routines, they are professionally disadvantaged.

In listing these questions – basic though they are – I encourage you to ask them if you believe they have not been adequately addressed (or that in not knowing the answers our professional capability will be somewhat compromised):

- Who is the year adviser/grade teacher to whom I am 'responsible'?
- Is there a colleague in my teaching area that I could/should meet with to give me some 'in-house' support today? Could you recommend someone?
- Bell times? Timetables? Map of school (with my teaching areas noted)?
- Copy of school discipline policy? Is there a summarized copy of the school's discipline policy devised for supply teachers? Some schools have a particular 'form' of discipline practice that is followed by all staff; it would be important to know this to enhance management consistency.
- Any crucial things I need to know at the outset? E.g. *time-out policy*? The time-out policy is crucial in one's daily supply teaching role. In 'challenging schools' the right and (at times) the need to exit a very disruptive, or aggressive, student is mandatory. We need to know that when a student is *repeatedly* disruptive we will be supported (without 'blame') with colleague back-up in the exit/time-out of such students (p. 90).

Supporting our classroom discipline

Such a plan also needs to be supported by thoughtful use of:

1 core routines such as corridor settling, seating 'plans', settling a class, cues for questions/discussion, noise levels, etc. (see Chapter 5);
2 collegial back-up for possible time-out situations (p. 89ff) and due process for discipline beyond the classroom;
3 appropriate follow-up of students by the supply teacher (beyond the classroom context) (p. 79, 80).

Survival strategies

No doubt many teachers have used survival strategies such as 'rewards': sweets, activities and games. ('If we can finish our work we can all go outside for a game'; 'trinkets for the natives'). Far be it for others to judge the probity of such strategies; there are some occasions when this may be the most reasonable way to cope with a very fractious class for a single day.

The problem comes when supply teachers frequently, easily and characteristically use such strategies. If 'rough behaviour modification' is used, it is important not to express it as a bribe or a threat: '*If* you're all good we will . . . ' or '*Unless* you're well behaved and get the work done we won't have any treats!'

When we're pressured, when we stare at a demanding lesson plan that seem miles away from our comfort zone, we're probably on safer, saner, ground to teach one of our standard, 'successful' lessons (within that broad curriculum/age area). Most regular teachers will appreciate that on such occasions, one-off occasions, 'we felt it wiser (for students and ourselves as supply teachers) to pursue a word game and an achievable writing activity, than seek to engage an involved lesson on "beginning" Haiku poetry or "third-world poverty in light of current globalization economics" . . . with a Year 9 class'. This is even more prudent if the 'roulette wheel' has spun you a known harder-than-average class.

It will be important to leave a note to that effect ('I felt it wiser, more prudent to . . . the students seemed to enjoy the activity (briefly spell out what you did). I enjoyed our time together . . . ' ('Well – sort of' – is what you're tempted to say.)

5

Core routines: what you establish you establish

There are two invaluable rules for a special correspondent – travel light and be prepared. Have nothing which in a case of emergency you cannot carry in your own hands.

(Evelyn Waugh, *in Scoop*)

In this section I want to address the basic, but crucial, routines that are necessary with every class in every lesson. Rather than merely hope that students will behave and work within routines, it will be necessary to 're-establish' these routines (if necessary) with each new group. This is best done by exercising one's leadership in an as-if way; 'as-if' such routines are normal, necessary and quite fair. In this our confident, expectant and positive manner will do more to establish our authority than any 'forced' loud voice or 'bossiness' on our part (pp. 28, 29).

The essential *core* routines and management issues we will need to consciously plan for are:

- corridor – settling/calming/'lining-up';
- settling a class within the classroom;
- initiating and sustaining whole-class attention;
- consciously dealing with early disruptions;
- transition from instructional to on-task time; partner-voice/movement patterns/teacher assistance/students without equipment/toilet breaks;
- planning for lesson closure;
- exit from room;
- cues for follow-up beyond classroom (where necessary), i.e. *how* we let a student(s) know we will need to 'speak to them . . . after class' or 'at recess in room ___'. (Even knowing which room to use for any lunch time follow-up is important; it demonstrates the supply teacher is 'in the know about the way things are done here').

Corridor settling

As supply teachers we often meet our students for the first time in the corridor, 'outside' the classroom. Effective behaviour management starts before we get into the classroom. Children may be restless, noisy, engaging in inappropriate calling out, even hassling the teacher. ('What you doing here?' 'Why are you here?' 'You our new teacher?') At secondary level students may effectively be behaving as if it's 'social time' rather than beginning class learning time: they'll be talking loudly; some will be restless; students – in some schools – will still be talking on their mobile phones, wearing Walkmans as they come into class; a few students may be testosteronically bonding (pushing, shoving, even play-punching or 'strangling').

It is worth having a brief, conscious, settling of the class 'outside' before 'taking' them in. Some schools have a normative policy of students entering the classroom without 'forming', 'grouping' or 'lining-up' outside the room – in that case we need to give some settling messages *as they come in.*

If there is a 'formal' lining-up the supply teacher can give a *group direction* to settle, 'remember where we're going', and a reminder/direction about coats/hats (even Walkmans) and phones (where necessary).

> As the Year 9 group forms outside the classroom Mr Smith stands near the door and scans the group, tactically ignores the calling-out questions ('What you doing here?' etc.). 'Settling down, thanks (. . .).' He consciously uses brief, tactical, pausing (. . .) to both engage and not rush the processing of what he is saying. He address the two lads 'play-punching' down the back. 'Fellas (. . .) fellas (. . .).' They look towards him. 'Recess time is over, remember we're going into a classroom. Thanks.' He briefly greets them all 'Morning, everyone.' It can help (in some schools) to use the more formal group appellation (4A, 6B, 10E). He mentions that he is their teacher – 'Mr Smith' – and that he will be taking Ms Davies's class today (always know the name of the regular teacher). He thus answers their calling out questions ('Who are you?') without acceding to their attentional behaviour by having outside class 'discussions' about who he is and why he is there.
>
> He notices a couple of ill-concealed mobile phones and a Walkman. 'I notice a few mobile phones down the back; and a Walkman' (he non-verbally cues the student to wind up the ear-buds). 'I also see some hats

on . . . remember we're going into a learning environment. Let's go in. Thanks.' His tone is confident, positive, expectant, matter of fact and this 'corridor-settling' has not taken long.

Some teachers will simply open the door and let noisy students in, with hats on, chewing gum, play-punching, making normative group settling/calming that much longer, that much more difficult.

Settling the class: initiating and engaging whole-class attention

If there is a normative seating plan it will be important to direct the students to their rows or table groups. It is also important not to engage in mini-discussions with students at the door (particularly at secondary level) about homework, projects, why 'you' are there, etc. It is enough to acknowledge the students, assure and defer their request ('I'll deal with that later in the lesson. For the time being please go to your seat. Thanks.') I've seen teachers have a 'back-log' of several students at the door while the class restlessly mills around them, holding up the beginning of class lesson time.

When seeking to engage (and sustain) whole-class attention it is important to stand at the front (centre) of the room, purposefully scanning the group as they 'take' their seats/places. As students arrive a little late it is important to briefly 'stop' them at the door, welcome them and direct them to their seats (or on the carpet at infant level). 'Welcome, I'm Mr Smith, please take your seat.' If they still have a coat/hat on, briefly remind them. 'You've got your coat/hat on.' Often an incidental descriptive reminder, or non-verbal cue (teacher touches own coat/head is enough. These may seem like small managerial points but they are important small managerial points that all add up to how our leadership is initially perceived by the class.

When standing at the front of the room to establish group attention it is important to stand 'formally' but relaxed, scanning the group and consciously acknowledging/affirming those students who are settling. (It does not help to sit at one's desk and seek to *initiate* and *sustain* group attention from there. It is important to be aware of one's overall body language and presence as a teacher-leader. If we pace up and down (at the front of the room while we seek to engage group attention) it will only serve to increase any motoric restlessness in our students as they will be *over-focusing* on the teacher's movement rather than on what he/she is saying.

It can help to non-verbally cue for class attention by 'tapping a glass' or, with infants, by cueing with a clapping 'signal'. *Verbal* cueing should always accompany non-verbal cues on the first meeting with a new class. It will also help to think about generic language: 'Guys . . .', 'Class . . .', '6A . . .', '9D . . .', 'Folks . . .', 'Everyone . . .'. 'Guys . . .' seems to be an accepted group generic (it's not my favourite but, then, I'm in my mid-fifties).

As we stand, relaxed, scanning the group, that – in itself – will be *cueing* for what we expect. Allow some *brief* tactical pausing (. . .) to allow processing of teacher direction and take-up of verbal cues. 'Settle down, everyone (. . .). Eyes and ears this way, thanks (. . .).' To *sustain* that initial, received attention (as eyes, ears and body language hopefully 'relax' in your direction) we might need to briefly 'discipline' the few students who are still chatting or talking across the room, or heavily seat-leaning or fiddling with pens or other *objets d'art*. if several students are fiddling with pens, small toys etc. it will be enough to give a *general*, whole-class, descriptive reminder, e.g. the teacher tactically pauses, scans the group, holds up a 'blocking hand' (to cue for 'stop and listen'): 'A number of students are fiddling with pens, or skateboards' (here the teacher looks directly and *briefly* at particular students). 'It's distracting; I'm trying to speak to our class.' It can help to then briefly, tactically, pause adding, 'Thanks'.

Again, the teacher's tone of voice and manner are very important. The tone is expectant, positive, almost matter of fact, as if it is the normal thing. Avoid a 'snappy', mean-spirited, 'nit-picky', bossy tone: 'I'm tough, I'm the boss here!' Also avoid using any sense of pleading, or 'please-be-reasonable-guys', voice (see Chapter 3).

Raised voices

When we characteristically, and frequently, use an overly raised voice to gain whole-class attention we reinforce that we only expect students to attend *when* we're very loud, which will mean that they, in effect, end up 'training us' to keep using a raised voice to 'seriously' gain whole-class attention. Our overly raised voice, or shouting, may even end up being a source of entertainment!

There are obviously times when a brief, firm, *raised* voice – even a 'sharp' raised voice – is essential; that is quite different from shouting (p. 51ff)

Student lateness

When students arrive late (while the teacher is engaged in whole-class learning time) it is important that the teacher cues for the student to stop, waits (briefly) near the door and then directs the student to his seat.

> Jayson arrives late. His body language is 'a bit cocky', he's got his coat on, bag over shoulder, baseball cap on. The rest of the class are in their seats, he's got an audience. He walks in (loudly) and goes to walk past the teacher; the teacher calls him back: 'Excuse me.' (The lad turns to face him.) 'What's your name, please?' (The tone is pleasant, relaxed, confident). 'Who are you?' The student's thinly concealed insouciance is *tactically* ignored by the teacher, he repeats the question. 'Welcome to our class. What's your first name?' 'Sean.' (It is mumbled.) 'Sean (. . .) welcome; I notice you're late.' (The teacher doesn't ask 'why' *at this stage*; it's probably not relevant plus he wants to see the student seated as soon as possible and resume the flow of the lesson. It's enough to *acknowledge* the lateness). 'There's a couple of seats over there.' The teacher points to the few spare seats.
> 'Don't want to sit there, I sit with . . . ' (here the student names his 'best' classmates; is he being genuine or, more likely, attentionally obtuse?)
> Rather than simply challenge, or argue, with the student the teacher *partially agrees/acknowledges* then *redirects* the student: 'I'm sure you do (. . .) those seats (where his mates are) are taken; there are some seats by the window. Thanks.' (He may add a possible option, 'We can organize a seat change later.' This can often 'mitigate' the direction in the ears of some students.)
> As the student takes his seat he mutters under his breath, 'Alright I'll sit there, I don't care.' The teacher *tactically* ignores the slouching, sighing, manner in which he goes to the seat. The teacher is, already, refocusing to the whole class and resuming the flow of the instructional phase of the lesson.

The teacher has kept the whole lateness issue to a minimum while still being 'relaxedly vigilant'. I have seen teachers who simply allow students to walk into class, walk in front of the teacher, *while* the teacher is talking (and ignoring the fact that the teacher is talking to the class group) and, en route to their seat, 'allow' the student to start a mini-chat or give out a 'playful punch' or two.

Some students who (having arrived late) will complain when you beckon them to 'stop' by the door. It is best to *tactically* ignore the whingeing tone, and quickly refocus. 'In our class, we knock and wait for our teacher to direct us to a seat. Thanks.' If they are really objectionable or verbally aggressive, we will need to make the immediate consequences of their behaviour clear to them: 'Sean, if you continue to argue with me about where to sit I'm going to have to ask you to leave our class for time-out.' As with *any* time-out options, the procedural process/plan needs to be clear in our mind *before* we go into our class(es) (p. 89ff).

Greeting the class at the first meeting

As with any new class a positive, greeting/welcome is fundamental. Avoid saying to the class something like: 'I'm just a supply teacher.' Better to say something like, 'My name is _____ . I'll be your teacher today while Ms/Mr _____ is away. I'm looking forward to working with you all' ('well sort of' – leave that bit out). Basic as it sounds it can even help to have one's name written up, in largish letters, on a cue card (affixed to the chalkboard). Avoid, too, going into long spiels about one's life as a teacher, and certainly avoid personal details; secondary students sometimes try to over-engage supply teachers on such issues.

In some schools the supply teacher is introduced to the class by the principal, deputy or year head. This both ratifies their professional status, gives visible moral support and telegraphs to the class that the senior staff member is 'cued-in' as it were. With known hard-to-manage classes it can help if the senior colleague 'stays-on' in the class for at least the establishment phase of the lesson to give visible, moral support. It will be important in such a situation for the senior colleague not to communicate (through body language or speech) that he/she is the 'real power' in the room and the supply teacher is the 'second-rate ' teacher. 'Good morning, everyone; let me introduce Ms Smith. As you know your regular teacher will be away for today (or . . .) having a deserved nervous breakdown (author's little joke). Ms Smith will be your teacher today.'

Even the way the senior colleague stands at the front of the room with their supply colleague can indicate professional support or 'superiority'. It can help if the senior colleague has a brief, precursory, chat about how they will do this (p. 101ff).

In some primary-age classes when the regular teacher is away and the class is 'covered' by a supply teacher, such a welcome is further ratified by nominated students who welcome the supply teacher on behalf of the grade/class (true!).

There are primary schools that have such a normative protocol. One of the students will stand up and say something like:

> On behalf of grade 6 we'd like to say welcome to you – Miss Snaggs – and we hope you'll enjoy working with us today. You probably know we have a student agreement, Miss, it's on the teacher's desk over there. It's the way we do things here, Miss. Thanks.' Some students even add a humourous 'good luck!' One can imagine how supported a supply teacher would feel, at the onset of the day, with such a welcome.
>
> At the close of the day a different student will get up and say something like: 'On behalf of grade 6 we'd like to say thanks for being here, we hope you enjoyed your time with us all.' I have heard of students who say they find such a 'good-bye' hard to give if they haven't had a 'nice' supply teacher. I'm sure such students gritted their teeth and did their best (wanting to say, perhaps, in closing 'and don't come back – please'.)

Learning names quickly

One of the natural difficulties of the one-day supply teacher is that often they do not know the children they teach. When their new, temporary teacher simply keeps saying 'You . . . yes you with your hand up' or 'You with the freckles and green hair' it can be annoying to the students. It is important in any teaching, particularly supply teaching, to make a conscious effort to learn student names quickly. A class roll and our memory is a basic start. (I often add brief written reminders as I'm marking the roll; sometimes asking a question of the student to briefly extend my memory bank while marking the roll.)

In some schools the class roll has photographs as well, which is a boon for learning names. Whenever I'm working with a new class at middle/upper primary level, I always ask a trustworthy-looking student to draw a seating plan of the room (a *simple* freehand plan) of desks –

referenced to the front/back of the room – and write the names of students at those desks/tables for *that* day. I have the said student doing this quietly (at the back of the room) during whole-class instructional time. Then, later in the on-task phase of the lesson, I use that as a prompt for learning and using the names when moving around the room.

It is important to always ask a student's name in any one-to-one dialogue; even in response to a question or contribution from a student during (say) instructional time. A brief and polite, 'What's your name, please?' is apposite. I always use a general cue prior to any class discussion: 'Before I start, whenever you share an opinion, ask a question or make a point, please let me know your first name it will help. Thanks.' If they forget to give me their name, I simply ask *before* responding to their question/contribution.

Sometimes a student will give a false name (it's *so* funny!). This has happened to me on a number of occasions. Sometimes another student will 'blow the gaff'. ('No way, Sir! He's not Fritz, he's Boris! He's winding you up!' – really?) There will always be dutiful peer laughter.

In one of my classes a student was continuing to call out. I *tactically* paused (. . .) looked at him and asked him his name. 'I've forgotten,' he answered as he looked around for the attentional guffaws. I let the laughter drop and briefly answered (non-sarcastically and even quietly) 'When you've remembered let me know (. . .). In the meantime remember the class rule for asking questions. Thanks.' With such a response it is important not to convey any sarcasm (tempting as it is!) or superiority. The tone is almost 'businesslike', not getting 'drawn', moving on to the real business of teaching/learning time.

There's no 'magic' to learning names; it might be associations of look/sound or (often) behaviour! It may be a simple 'shufti' at their class book or pencil case as you move around the room. I have noticed, too, that when I'm trying hard to remember a student's name, 'I'm trying to remember your name' is a more positive prompt than 'I've forgotten your name'. It is basically a conscious, willing, effort to engage and relate to 'our' students; even a greeting (where appropriate) in the corridor, in the playground, or at lunchtime will help.

The overly restless class

In some secondary school classes – and even some upper primary classes – you will probably come across a *very* restless class. It seems to take a good five minutes to 'settle them down'. I have had a number of classes like that over the years. There's no 'honeymoon period', no period of 'grace', in that first meeting. Half a dozen students are still chatting away, ignoring the teacher at the front of the room who is trying to gain some semblance of order and focus.

It can be tempting to shout the class into some sense of attention and focus – such a course nearly always results in the students merely laughing, which may see some teachers resort to early threats of dire consequences which can rarely be carried out (e.g. whole-class detentions). If the class does settle down as a result of a teacher's shouting ('Shut up!') it is at best a temporary settling. What is one to do then? Shout again (30 seconds to a minute) later?

I had such a class that I covered for a colleague one day. I hadn't worked with this Year 9 class before. They were restless enough in the corridor (p. 57), once inside the classroom they quickly 'reverted' (so it seemed) to their habituated behaviours. Three boys dived for the back row; two started some play-punching; the third tried to squeeze into an non-existent seat. Students were loudly talking to each other or across the room. A girl was standing by the window talking to some friends outside the classroom (students running late to another class). Several students were calling out to me at the front of the room.

On such occasions, instead of 'formally' starting the lesson, I leave the front of the room and move around establishing contact with each little group; asking for first names (and mostly getting their 'real' names, p. 62) and having brief chats about 'what sort of work they are doing at the moment in this class'. Approaching the young lads at the back, I said: 'Fellas, you're bonding again and I'm ready to begin our class in a few moments.' (I'd already spoken to them about their 'testosteronic-bonding' in the corridor). 'We just mucking around' (this is the most common reply I get from boys and is, no doubt, truthful in its way).

'I'm sure you are just mucking around, fellas.' (I've found that partial agreement often helps in such situations.) I asked their names. 'Andrew, Sean and Brett, I'm ready to start our class. Andrew, there's some spare seats over there.' I gestured. 'But I want a seat here.' I responded to his whinge with some more 'partial agreement. 'There's no spare seats here, Andrew, there's seats over there. Thank you.' The 'incidental' direction was clear. I walked away giving him some take-up time and had a chat to the girl by the window. 'Excuse me . . . (she turned) what's your name, please?'

'What?'

'Your name, please.'

'Belinda.' She gave a 'tut' and sigh (Oh my – I had intruded on her tête-à-tête with some girls *outside* [through the classroom window]). 'Belinda, you are out of your seat, the bell has gone I'm about to start our class.' This is a description of obvious reality and an implied direction ('You know you should be in your seat').

'I was just talking to my friends.' (What did she think this was – an extended playtime?) I didn't argue, or berate her. ('Listen I don't give a damn about your friends, just shut it and get into your seat now!') 'I'm about to start the class Belinda, there are seats over there.' I gestured. The girls outside moved off to class. I walked away from Belinda, to give her some take-up time and en route to the front of the room had some more mini-chats with the more restless students.

This 'class-circuit' took about four minutes; I had learned quite a few names. Going to the front of the classroom I stood front centre looking (and largely feeling) ready. I Scanned the room, waited 10–15 seconds and, now, formally began: 'Settling down, everyone (. . .). Looking this way and listening.' Several or more did just that, I acknowledged, 'Sean . . . Dean, Melissa, Belinda, Zoohar, Mahmoud.' The more restless students I cued again, 'Several students need to be looking this way and listening.' As they did I briefly thanked them. The class was settling down, I could 'feel' the residual calmness. I was now able to use my relaxed, 'normal' speaking voice.

'Good morning everyone, (. . .). Welcome to another session but with a 'new' teacher. My name is . . . '

Another teaching day.

If the class is *significantly* unresponsive to any of our cues or directions for whole-class attention we should resist the banging of three-foot rulers, or loud shouting (tempting of course). On such occasions it is important to send for senior teacher assistance as soon as possible (p. 90) rather than just start 'teaching' through disparate attentional noise. Such teacher behaviour may give the illusion of 'surviving' but only reinforces that it is OK for half the class to effectively ignore the teacher. Hopefully, the school will have a policy of a 'common establishment phase' practice with a known *very* restless class. On these occasions a senior teacher will team-teach with the colleague for the first 10–15 minutes and then casually leave the classroom with an 'I'll be back a little later'.

This 'shared establishment' can often give a sort of 'credibility by proxy' (Rogers, 2000b) and is essential when a supply teacher takes up a known hard class for an extended supply cover.

Seating/grouping plans

Students sometimes give supply teachers a hard time when it comes to seating arrangements ('who sits with whom', 'how seating is arranged' etc. It will help to check if the regular teacher has a set seating plan for a given class. If not, we can check with the year head whether it will be appropriate to seek to change the 'seating plan' for that day (at primary).

If the seating arrangements are clearly counter-productive for some students it will be important to consider how to redirect seating placement for some students during class time. Yes, the students will complain and we should, obviously, give a 'choice' before directing certain students to sit away from each other (in order to get the class work done). 'If you continue to work noisily/if you cannot complete the set work because you are continuing to talk, I'll have to have you working separately (think about it).'

In a primary class we may find ourselves having to rearrange the seating plan between class periods if necessary. It will help if we let the students know beforehand and, *if possible*, enlist the support of a senior colleague.

Whenever we change seating arrangements – when teaching on a 'day-cover' – we need to do so only as a 'last resort' and with a decisive, positive emphasis that this 'will help us with our learning time today.'

If the supply teacher has a long-term leadership role with the class it may help to regroup the whole-class seating arrangements – perhaps more 'formally' in rows. If the first few lessons/sessions see the students highly restless, attentional and off-task it may well be the result of who they sit with, and the physical seating arrangements. I have observed classes where table groups are 'over-stacked' – six to eight friends on one table, one or two on another (the 'cools' and the 'un-cools'). Simply allowing students to sit in groups does not guarantee co-operative learning behaviours.

Regrouping a fractious upper primary or secondary group is not easy. I have found it helpful to partly engage their co-operation by letting them know 'there will be a change of seating plan' starting next _____ ' (next class period, or next day at primary). When this announcement is made it will be helpful to have a senior colleague present.

'As your teachers we are concerned about the level of noise during class work time, we're also concerned about students being off-task – not really getting much class work done. We believe a change of seating will help. We will be rearranging the class seating in rows (as from _____). We want you to write down two names of students you know will not hassle you, or make it difficult for you to do your class work and who will support you . . . We will use your suggestions in the final seating arrangements. Thanks, Mr Smith . . . and Mr Rogers.'

When students call out

Talking while the teacher is talking, and calling out are among the most commonly cited distracting and disruptive behaviours during whole-class instruction/teaching. It will help to preface all whole-class teaching and discussion times with a brief (and positive) rule reminder. 'Before we start folks, I want to remind you of our class rule for question/discussion time . . . ' It will obviously help to have a visual rule poster up high on the chalkboard as a visual prompt/aide-memoire (p. 69). It is also helpful to remind the whole class that any individual student's questions or contribution is not a one-to-one dialogue with the teacher that simply gives the rest of the class the opportunity to privately chat. An individual's response or contribution in class discussion is a contribution for all to hear.

It will naturally help if the teacher does not have extended dialogues with any one student during class discussion/question time (at least until one gets to know the mix of personalities!). With upper primary classes it will be enough to remind students of the basic courtesy of 'One at a time, thanks' and then reinforce that fair expectation (cum rule) when an individual does talk over another student, or butts in, while a fellow student is trying to ask a question or make a point.

Avoid accepting a kind of 'norm' that sees the teacher trying to talk 'through' students chatting (while the teacher is talking), or several students calling out (even with their hands up) and then accepting their contribution/question. All that does (obviously) is reinforce that it is OK to virtually ignore the teacher during whole-class instruction. If, further, we accept such behaviour one day and try to clamp down on another day it only habituates teacher inconsistency about appropriate (and fair) behaviour.

When students call out severally or individually it will be enough to say something like 'A number of students (avoid saying 'all of you') are calling out . . . remember our class rule, thanks.' When students do put their hands up it is important to acknowledge the individual particularly if you want them to wait for a minute. If several students have their hands up obviously cue the whole class: 'I can see several hands up. Sean, Craig, Elisa, Zoohar . . . I'll get back to you one at a time; hands down. Thanks. Sean first . . . '

I have worked with teachers who have habituated repeated and frequent distracting behaviours (such as those above) by not consciously addressing them in the first instance of their occurring.

Introduce your rules: first session, first day

After a brief introduction to yourself it will be crucial to introduce the rules you will be working with that day, week or term. The least helpful introduction to a new class group is to ask the students 'what rules they use in class'.

'Your regular teacher has rules for your class, the rules I have brought along today are the same as those that Ms /Mr/Miss _____ has made with you.' Any differences between 'your' rules and the class rules will be minor and if 'challenged' (by older students) it is enough to say: 'These rules as you can see here (here the supply teacher points back to the published rules-posters on the chalkboard/whiteboard) will be our rules for today. Thanks.'

(Always refer to their teacher by regular name Ms/Mr/Miss _____ or first name if that is the preferred usage.)

It is important to take your 'own' rules along simply because some teachers do not have any established or visibly 'published' rules in their

classroom. The rules may be ambiguous, or negatively stated. (e.g. 'Do *not* call out in class', 'Don't run in the room', 'Don't chew gum'). By taking your 'own' rules you demonstrate a confident expectation about behaviour and learning *while* you are with them. It is crucial, of course, that in establishing such rules the tone communicated is positive, expectant almost matter of fact – you are stating expectations (via the rules) which are based on fair rights and responsibilities.

The rules need to be few in number, positive in expression (wherever possible) and focused on desired (and fair) behaviour. If a negative expression is used it can be balanced by a positive expression, e.g. 'In our class we put our hands up (for questions/discussions) without calling out.' Or, even shorter, 'Hands up without calling out – thanks.'

A fundamental feature of a supply teacher's discipline plan is their ability to engage teaching, learning and co-operative behaviour within fair, positive rules.

The key to the rules (at any age level) is that they are based on normative rights:

- *The right to learn here* (without undue, unfair, distraction or disruption).
- *The right to have one's person and property respected here./The right to fair treatment here.*
- *The right to feel safe here.*

Each *core right* implies *core responsibilities*. The *purpose* of rules is to protect these rights, encourage responsibilities and give a common reference for any discipline when rules are infringed or abused.

The wording and phrasing of the rules is very important. At infant, lower primary level it can help to have headings that state the expected behaviours with some simple 'cartoon' drawings.

> To learn well here:
> – We use our 'inside voices' in class.
> – We walk in our classroom.
> – We help each other to learn.
> – We put our hands up without calling out.
> – We always pack up at our table groups.

With older students (upper primary and secondary) it can help to have the core right prefacing the rule. For example

---

WE ALL HAVE A RIGHT TO LEARN.
To learn well here we: (then list the key expectations about *learning well*).

- Get to class on time.
- Settling quickly at workplace/desks.
- Hands up for questions/discussions.
- Partner-voice/co-operative talk in learning time.

Thanks for your co-operation.
   Mr/Ms _____

Even with secondary students I find that a few simple cartoons can 'lift' the stated words, and can give a visual prompt.

Student behaviour agreements

Some class groups (particularly at primary-age level) have *student behaviour agreements* negotiated by the grade teacher with the class in the establishment phase of the year (Rogers, 2000a). Copies of these are made available to the supply teacher so they can engage their leadership of the class (and their discipline where necessary) *within* that agreement. It is worth asking, on arrival at the school, if there is such an 'agreement' or 'class code'. Such agreements are more than a list of rules and consequences; they are a published agreement (often signed by the students) that forms a basis for shared understandings about behaviour and learning in that class, that school.

Transitions

In the transition between 'instructional'/whole-class teaching time and 'on-task/learning time it is important to remember that any task-focus instructions be given visually not just auditorily. It is also important to not give half a dozen task items. Students will often say (later):

Student	'What do we have to do, Miss?'
Teacher	'Weren't you listening?!'

What is crystal clear to us may not be clear to all our students. By visually writing up the key tasks, clearly, sequentially and briefly taking the students through the three or four key points/tasks we increase the task clarity for all.

Managing noise levels during on-task learning time

It is natural that noise levels of students rise when they move into the on-task phase of the lesson. Some students will become more motorically restless ('wandering'), engage in task avoidance or hassle other students (for 'socializing' fun); other students will pester the teacher for assistance or even plain attention ('notice *me!*').

On the very first meeting with a new class it is important to clarify appropriate, expected (and necessary) 'noise levels' *before* moving into the on-task learning time.

At the close of the whole-class instructional/teaching/discussion, it is important to:

- clarify the learning tasks, preferably with visual prompts, key points written on the board or 'mind-mapping' on the board (when appropriate), even a pre-prepared chart with learning requirements for that lesson or activity. The least effective 'prompts' are auditory (just telling students what they have to do) – or giving too many auditory task instructions;
- remind the students about 'noise levels' and 'work-talk' ('partner-voices' or 'inside voices' for younger students);
- remind the students about 'co-operative talk' (talk focused on supporting *our learning time* together by talking *about* the work *with* their classmates);
- clarify how they can get teacher assistance appropriately;
- make clear what to do when they have completed the set task (*always* plan ahead for 'early finishers' or those who rush the work). I find it helpful to have a menu of options for older students. Make sure there are some enjoyable options such as reading chapter 2 of the Harry Potter novel (or whatever). Certainly some user-friendly, self-contained worksheets won't go amiss here;
- make sure you have a box of spare pens, rulers, pencils, sharpeners, erasers, blank/lined paper (*and* your own chalk/whiteboard markers [check them]/chalkboard eraser, etc.).

These core routines can be written up on a pre-prepared poster with key words to act as a visual prompts/cues. It looks, then, as if the 'supply' teacher is well prepared and consciously focused for on-task learning time.

Of course, having routines (and rules p. 68) is never enough by itself. The skills of positive teaching, management and discipline mean we monitor, maintain, remind, encourage and discipline *within* those routines, so we establish a positively *normed* environment.

Working with a Year 9 science class on a one-off lesson I discussed with them the importance of 'partner-voices' and 'co-operative talk'. Raising the issue I asked: 'What comes into your head when I use the term *partner-voice* in terms of our class-learning time?' Several students called out. *Tactically* ignoring those students I reminded the class about calling out. Scanning the group and giving a brief rule-reminder was enough '(. . .)

Remember our class rule for asking questions. Thanks.' ('Thanks' can add a positive expectational tone to the rule reminder.)

The student responses about 'partner-voice' included: 'eye-contact' (to the person next to you/partner); 'first name'; keep the voice *level* down/soft/quiet; talking with/to the person next to you not the person on the *other* side of the room (that one was also raised by me). We discussed how 28 students, plus two teachers (I was mentoring with a colleague) is a lot of people in a small place; hopefully, all with a common aim – shared learning. We went on to discuss how co-operative talk can help us achieve that aim ('talk focused on each of us making some effort to support each other, and our teacher, in the shared learning'). One of the more prosaic definitions of 'co-operative talk' I have heard is 'anything that doesn't easily, or quickly, focus on *Neighbours, Home and Away*' (or some other favourite television show).

During this discussion I had a student record the key descriptive points about 'partner-voice' on the board. These became our 'litmus test' of 'partner-voice' and 'co-operative talk'. When I am working with a class longer term my colleagues and I make up a simple poster with the key words as a visual aide-memoir. To monitor and give feedback on their 'partner-voices' (as a class group) I used a feedback graph (Rogers, 2000a). On the horizontal axis the on-task learning time is divided into three- or five-minute sections. The vertical axis is divided into 10 sections. Zero is silence, number two is whisper zone, number five is upper limit of 'partner-voice' – over five it's *too loud*. Ten is 'House of Commons' level!

Visual prompts for partner-voice are very helpful at infant and middle-primary level. One such prompt I have seen is where the teacher has several coloured flags (visible from the back of the class). Each flag denotes a level, or kind, of voice. The white flag is hands up (without calling out); one at a time. The green flag denotes 'our quiet working voices', the pink flag our 'whispering voices'.

Over 20 years ago I developed a similar noise monitor: a large 15-inch circle of cardboard comprising three segments with three colours denoting levels and use of 'voice':

- The white third of the colour circle denotes hands up without calling out; one at a time; listen when others speak; and wait your turn.

- The next colour (the green third) denotes 'quiet working voices' or 'inside voices' or 'partner-voices'.
- The orange third denotes a warning, a reminder, that the class needs to stop and think about what 'voice' they should be using. Combined with positive encouragement and correction it can be a useful aide-memoire for the class. Correction can include simple reminders such as, 'We're in white zone now', 'Remember, everyone, what we need to be doing when we're in green zone'. A split pin arrow stays on the colour part of the 'noise-monitor' for that 'phase' of the lesson (see Rogers, 2000b).

If the regular teacher has his/her own cues for 'inside-voices'/'working noise' and such cues are positive and reasonably effective, these should be part of the 'information pack' provided to the supply teacher on arrival to the school.

At infant (lower primary) level it is not uncommon for the regular teacher to use a particular clapping signal, a bell, a raised hand (to cue students to raise their right hand for a 'domino' settling effect). These are all typical non-verbal cues for whole-class attention and focus.

In one school I worked in an infant teacher had a simple 'Simon says' cue for her class. 'We put our hands on our head to show we come in here to think.' (Here the teacher models by putting her hands briefly on her head.) 'We also think with our hearts.' (Here the teacher folds her hand briefly over her heart.) 'We relax our body.' (Here the teacher breathes out as she rests her hands briefly on her shoulders in a downward motion.) 'And, last of all, we put our hands in our lap to show we are ready.' In time these few, brief, visual cues become the 'Simon says' norm for quiet and ready during carpet time. Again it will help if the supply teacher knows these cues (and uses them) to enhance 'continuity'.

Task avoidance/refusal

Students will task-avoid for a number of reasons: disorganized behaviour, boredom, inability to understand or cope with the work, or attention (wanting the teacher frequently to come back to them and 'assure', 'approve', 'notice', etc.).

Some of these 'reasons' one can address through one's general management, e.g.: fine-tuning/adapting of task; avoid completely renegotiating a task. Our awareness of demands for attention will be important: 'Craig (. . .) when you are back in your seat working then I'll come over and have a look at your work' (this to an attentional, wandering, student). Some say the work is boring: 'Gees, Miss, we done fractions stacks of times. This is boooring.'

'You could well be right Manuel, sometimes we have to do boring things; this is the work we're all doing today. I'll help to make it a little less boring. Come on.'

This often meets with a resigned sigh and very slow getting back 'to work'.

If the student's time-on-task work is being adversely affected by sitting with another student, we can consider arranging for him to work somewhere else in the room, an approach best prefaced with a 'choice'. 'You seem to be having some problems *really* getting started Melissa. I've seen you having lots of talking time and not working. I can arrange for you to work separately. I'll come back and see how you're going later.'

'You can't make me do the work.' Sometimes a student will exhibit some 'cocksparrow' attentional power ('Look at me; the supply teacher can't make me do nothing' – which, of course, is true). Rather than giving the student what he wants – a power exchange, 'You will – I'll make you' 'You'll go to detention!' ('I don't care . . . !') – we need to make the consequences clear. 'I'm sure you are able to do the work. If you can't, I'll help. If you choose not to do the work, I'll need to see you after the lesson. Think about it.'

'Can't make me!'

'Of course I can't make you, Nathan, I'm not even going to try (the teacher says this quietly, decisively, relaxedly – Nathan is no threat). If you continue to choose not to work I'll have to follow it up later with you and the year adviser' (though avoid adding 'and he's got a lot more power than me and *he'll* make you suffer').

We cannot make students work. In some secondary schools as long as the student is not hassling other students I will leave them with:

- the offer of assistance at any time;
- the deferred consequence of choosing, purposefully, not to 'work'. A deferred consequence will normally entail some kind of 'stay-back', or follow-up later that day (pp. 79, 80, 83, 86ff).

Lesson closure and exit from the classroom

As noted earlier, many aspects of one's behaviour management appear 'small' when noted in isolation from the many aspects of classroom discipline in a single lesson.

I have seen many teachers (more so at secondary level) 'allow' a class to 'bolt' at the first sound of the recess bell! It can be irritating to enter a classroom where the previous teacher has allowed the class to leave with the seats and tables all awry, with little bits of litter like confetti, etc. One can hardly blame the students. If we, as supply teacher, merely let the class effectively 'do a runner' we reinforce the attitude that we don't care how they leave, or what state we (as teacher-leader) allow the classroom to be left in.

Like most aspects of behaviour management some prior, conscious, planning can help: finishing the lesson early enough to allow for collection/return of materials; a brief recap of the lesson (where appropriate) or even a brief classroom discussion of learning connections made that period; a reminder about residual litter, furniture straightening, an orderly 'exit' and a positive ending and 'goodbye' (for now).

Whenever I'm teaching an upper primary class, or secondary class, I write the acronym **dtncaft** on the board: 'do the next class a favour, thanks'. At the close of the last period for the day I drop out the 'n' (e.g. 'do the cleaner a favour, thanks, **dtcaft**')

Under the acronym (dtncaft) I write the three obvious reminders:

1 **SF** straighten the furniture
2 **RLP** pick up any residual litter please; and
3 **RBR** we leave row by row (or **TGBTG** table group by table group).

A brief explanation to underscore and explain *why* we're going out 'row by row' will help. 'Remember, folks, it's easy to just race off leaving the classroom furniture messed up. Let's take half a minute (not long!) to do the next class a favour. And by leaving row by row we make sure that we show basic consideration to each other and the other classes next door. Thanks.' This 'routine' doesn't take long. Some students (say Year 8s and 9s) will whinge at the RBR ('row by row') but that can be *tactically* ignored.

Of course we need to communicate this basic routine in a positive, confident, tone.

If some students do 'race off' towards the door, as the bell goes, it is worth firmly (not nastily) calling them back. A raised voice (not shouting!): 'Stop, at the door (. . .). Stop, back inside (. . .) back inside, thanks (name the students if you can remember) . . . ' We will often need to briefly repeat part of the instruction. Seventy per cent of the class will probably be sitting or standing at their seats 'watching', 'waiting', as it were, to see how this little 'defining moment' pans out.

Commonly the three, or five, students who had made the rapid dash walk back to their tables muttering – whingeing, sighing, under their

breath ('This is a repressive regime!'). Poor things, we've taken a minute off their recess.

A *brief* reminder to the whole class about how we leave is appropriate. 'When you're settled I'll explain (. . .).' (Allow some settling as you visually scan the group.) 'This is not a detention, folks, it's a *brief* reminder to us all. In our class we leave without running, or trying to get to the door first. This time I want you to remember what I said earlier – row by row. Thanks.' This whole-class reminder does not take long and it reaffirms the intent of our positive leadership. The teacher then signals a row by a student's name, and the class leaves in a more orderly fashion (a few will still be engage in *sotto voce* sighing and whingeing ('Gees, what kind of class is this?').

It will help if the teacher stands by the door to at least visually give a last goodbye, 'See you again'. Some students will return a pained frown: 'You coming back again?' We'll return that one with a firm, smiling whisper: 'You could be in luck, Travis.'

If a few students bolt off even after we've called them back, we just 'cut our losses', record the names and pass the concern on to a senior colleague (to enhance the overall certainty of fair consequential reminders). It may even be possible to do some follow-up yourself (see below).

'Just' because we are supply teachers it does not mean we do not exercise the kind of positive behaviour management that all effective teachers normally exercise.

Follow-up/follow-through with students (beyond classroom context)

It may be argued that because a supply teacher may *only* be at a school for a day they need not follow-up classroom incidents one to one with a student (e.g. rudeness, significant task avoidance, brief mediation between students in conflict, following up on time-out *when initiated by the supply teacher*).

Regular teachers can, naturally, get annoyed when the supply teacher *merely* passes on a list of complaints about an individual, or class, telling the regular teacher they 'should punish Jayson because . . . '. If the supply teacher leaves *all* follow-up to the regular class/grade teacher it will reinforce in the eyes of the students (yet again?) that the supply teacher has no substantial teacher/leadership 'status'.

It is difficult to follow up and follow through with students in a busy day-cover of the teacher – particularly as a secondary supply teacher. As a primary supply teacher follow-up is somewhat easier, and very important. Some issues, some behaviour concerns, will need that extra after-class time to clarify your concerns about a behaviour or a learning issue. This follow-up establishes both our concern and the appropriate consequential follow-through. Such follow-up/follow-through may be as basic as a brief chat, a 'task-consequence' (cleaning up 'mess'/finishing a work task), a more protracted 'interview' (10 minutes) or a subject-teacher 'detention' at lunch time.

Some fundamental protocols about follow-up/follow-through

1 Check if there is a school policy about stay-back/after-class consequences.
2 Consider the ethical probity of a male teacher conducting an after-class one-to-one interview with a *female* student. Apart from a brief 'clarifying word' after class, any longer chat/interview (about behaviour or learning concerns) is best conducted with a female colleague present and organized with year-adviser permission.
3 When speaking with a student on a one-to-one basis it will help to 'tune into' how they are feeling (probably a bit uptight, annoyed, even angry; some will be a little 'anxious' even 'confused' as to why you have asked *them* to stay back after class, 'Me, what did I do?').
'Adam you're probably feeling a bit annoyed that I've asked you to stay back after class . . . ' (This *brief* tuning in can put the student a little at ease and 'telegraph' your concern.) What we need to convey as their 'new' (if temporary) teacher is the *certainty* of fair consequential due process. If we simply use follow-up for some kind of 'emotional payback' we'll effectively lose any workable relationship with the student for the rest of the teaching day, e.g.: 'You could be outside now couldn't you eh? But no. You had to be stupid didn't you? What did I say? Didn't I say that if you didn't stop all your talking and get your work done I'd keep you back – didn't I say that?! And what did you say, eh? You said you didn't care – you're caring now aren't you?' (I've heard teachers talk like that.) It is the *certainty* rather than merely the severity of the consequence, that hopefully will teach the child the reasonable and fair connection between behaviour and consequence.
4 Refer to the behaviour, issue or task you have 'kept them back' for. This is not an attack on the student but a reference to the fact that it was his/her *behaviour* that was disruptive, unfair, inconsiderate, 'rude': 'Jayson I'm really concerned about the *way* you spoke to me in class – several times – when you said things like . . . ' (be *briefly* specific about what it is they said, or did). It may help to 'mirror' their behaviour to them. Ask them if you can 'show them' what it looks like when they 'call out loudly', 'speak rudely', 'ignore you by turning away when you

Teacher_____

Class_____ Date_____

Think about what happened in class time . . .

1. What happened (what I did, my behaviour) . . . ?

_____

_____

_____

2. What rule was broken? _____

_____

_____

_____

3. What do you have to say about what happened? (What is your side
   of the story?)

_____

_____

_____

4. What can I do to make things better, fix things up?

_____

_____

_____

speak . . . '. 'Mirroring' can be a simple, *brief* way of kinaesthetically connecting with a student. Keep such mirroring brief; never humiliate. Use it to clarify and illustrate the aspect of the student's behaviour you want to focus on. It will also help to physically 'step back' to become the adult who can now say, '*That's* what it looks (or sounds) like when you . . . ' (point back to the vacated 'space').

If it is a 'task-consequence' we keep the student back for (cleaning up mess; finishing a work task; even putting chairs back before they tried to race off at lunch recess), it will be enough to point out what wasn't done and what needs to be done now ('Won't take long . . . and that's the way we do things in *our* class, Troy . . . '). Direct them to the task, give them some 'take-up time' (don't stand over them as it were) and thank them at the close. It will help to tactically ignore any surliness *while* they're doing the 'onerous' task.

5 Where appropriate invite the student's right of reply: 'What do you have to say about . . .?' If they become defensive, or start discounting their behaviour ('others did stuff, too', 'I'm not the only one', 'just joking anyway') it will help to reframe: 'In our class it is not a joke to do/or say . . . ' (be specific). 'Even if others did call out (be specific), at the moment I'm speaking to you about the many times that you called out and argued with me.'

   If you are conducting a lunch-time stay-back/detention, it may be appropriate to direct the student to fill in a right of reply pro forma, with some focused questions such as: '*What happened* (to cause you to be in detention)'? '*What rule* (or right – this for secondary age students) *was broken* (or affected by your behaviour)?' '*What's your side of the story*?' (or 'What do you think?') '*What can you do to fix things up*?' Many schools build such pro formas into their discipline/welfare policies. Point out to the student that a copy of this will stay with the regular class teacher and the year head. I am always willing, too, to make a copy for the student if they wish.

6 It will also help to briefly relate their behaviour back to the school/or classroom code of behaviour.

7 Always separate amicably in any one-to-one follow-up; even at the end of a brief after-class chat. Avoid the easy temptation to go over the issue again and get into a last warning lecture: 'If you do that again, Troy, not only will you be staying back *again*, I'll make sure you go on

detention *and* I'll contact your mother – alright?'

(a) Remember if you are a primary teacher you will be teaching this student again, later, that day. Or if you ever teach at that school again that child will remember.
(b) We want the class 'tribal tom-toms' to work in our favour. This doesn't mean we're soft, or that we simply acquiesce; it means we are respectful and professional in our consequential discipline.
(c) Any follow-up process we engage in should be written up and passed on to the grade leader/year adviser and a copy left for the grade teacher.

Notebook it

My colleagues and I have found it helpful to have a notebook to record names of students we need to follow up at the close of a lesson. The notebook is both an aide-memoire and a visible cue to the whole class that we take follow-up (beyond the classroom) seriously. Many, many times I have finished a first lesson with a new class and almost the last thing before I direct the class to leave is a brief recourse to 'the notebook'. 'Before we leave, I need to speak to Damien and Troy briefly after class.' Most students whinge: 'What for – what did I do – nothing!!' I find it helpful not to engage with a student at that point (in front of the class) regarding their protestations about 'keeping them back'.

At secondary level the stay-back after-class chat is often brief – just enough time to let them know you want to see them briefly (five minutes) at lunch time (name a room; say, the year head's room).

There's no need to get the notebook out with a dramatic 'police-person' flourish; just a relaxed normalcy that *this* teacher, *this* day will be following up on an issue that matters.

One supply colleague (Ros) notes that when she made the effort to 'follow-up after lessons'.

It made an impression on both pupils and staff. It also helped me to focus on individuals rather than classes in difficult lessons at secondary level, and to remember that not *all* the pupils were behaving badly. I wrote lots of notes to form tutors for help in chasing up missing books, homework and so on. Some of them did not appreciate this but I did get support from others which, in turn, made a difference in the behaviour of pupils in lessons (they know I know that the form teacher knows . . .) . . . ' (Rogers, 2000b, p. 128).

Duty of care beyond the classroom

One of the problems of managing behaviour in non-classroom settings is that some teachers exercise no duty-of-care 'vigilance' beyond the classrooms. They walk past students engaged in vigorous pushing and shoving in corridors, ignore basketball being played in corridors and ignore students going through non-student thoroughfares. I've heard teachers say things like 'but I'm not on corridor duty' or 'wet day duty' or 'lunch duty'. 'Oh well I won't bother speaking to the students about eating in the corridor; or running, or going through a no-student thoroughfare . . . I don't want to make a fuss.' When we leave our class-rooms we are in effect 'on duty' and need to exert some *relaxed* vigilance – even as a supply teacher!

In one of the schools where I was an on-going mentor I was walking down the corridor from the administration area. As I approached the door through to the main corridor (which had a sign affixed 'No Student Thoroughfare') I saw a small group of students heading towards the (no student access) door. One of the girls said (as she saw me through the glass door), 'Sh*t it's him.' and they turned and walked the other way. I'm not nasty but they knew I'd be *relaxedly vigilant* in addressing their behaviour.

The *basic* pre-emptive necessities

In detailing these I don't want to sound 'grandmother-sucking-eggs-ish'. Yet I have seen supply teachers either forget, not seriously consider or even ignore these basic hallmarks of effective teaching practice. They are fundamental to our professionalism.

- Be at class on time; be ready to receive the class (especially at secondary level) 'in the corridor' or 'outside the class' – whatever the appropriate entry-to-class procedure is.
- Have the class attendance roll at hand (check through before class, if there's time, for pronunciation of names). Rehearse 'difficult-sounding' names (p. 62ff). Supply teachers often find it helpful to use simple

sticker name tags on which they can write students' names. This can be a useful novelty even in middle school.

- Consciously learn students' names (quickly, even in the one day).
- Have some brief corridor settling (if there is a 'line-up' policy). Address hat/coats etc. (p. 67ff).
- Make sure that little time is lost in finding seats – plan for this (it won't just happen).
- *Always* have spare chalk/duster/whiteboard markers to hand (again this is essential at secondary school level). It looks so unprofessional to see a teacher shuffling and 'umming/ahhing' at the front of the classroom. 'Oh, um, has anyone seen the chalk – um – could someone go to the class next door and get me some chalk, please?' (Half a dozen students race off out of the room to help. 'I'll go, I'll go!').
- Have a box of spare pens, rulers, pencils, paper (etc.) for those students who 'forget'. (p. 47, 48).
- Have spare worksheets, 'busy work' and some well-known, simple, enjoyable games that the whole class can enjoy and engage in quickly (association games, quizzes, number games, etc.).
- Have some worksheets (age-related) for students with special needs; worksheets (in the key subject areas you teach). A range of 'stickers' won't go astray.
- Have 'your own' rules with you (just in case) (p. 68ff).
- Discuss your expectations for behaviour and learning (in a *brief* and *positive* way) at the outset (p. 11ff, 68ff).
- Have a positive start to the first session (p. 58ff, 61ff).
- Know the bell/break times and how long the class periods are (don't rely on students telling you!). This is basic, I know, but I have seen supply teachers stymied by older students who 'cut' class early (a personal timer watch can help have a planned lesson closure and dignified ending and exit from the class – p. 76ff).
- Check if you have any duties other than class teaching, e.g. 'spares' (cover class duty at secondary), wet day duty, lunch duty (are you expected to stay if the primary class goes to a specialist teacher?).
- Are you expected to stay back after school if there is a staff meeting?
- Are you required to leave a report for the grade/subject teacher? It is good form to leave a positive note anyway.
- *Always* leave the room as tidy as (or more tidy than) you found it.

6

Behaviour consequences

*A few years ago I met an old professor at the University of Notre Dame.
Looking back on his long life of teaching he said – with a funny twinkle
in his eye, 'I have always complained that my work was constantly
interrupted until I slowly discovered that my interruptions were my
work.'*

(Henri Nouwen)

If a supply teacher is going to be accepted as a fellow professional (within
the colleague team for that day, that week) they need to be able to exercise
normal behaviour consequences *within the school's discipline policy*.

While the supply teacher may be constrained somewhat by the fact they
only teach a class for one day (even a few periods as in secondary schools)
it is important that they convey to students that they have the right to
exercise consequential discipline and will, where necessary, carry it out.

In this they will need the support of their colleagues in:

- clarifying the normal range of consequences (including brief stay-back
  sessions one-to-one after class – p. 79ff);
- knowing what 'incident report sheets' to use for referral of a discipline
  issue beyond the supply teacher's reasonable discipline duty-of-care;
- awareness of the normal protocols of follow-up consequences *beyond*
  classroom settings (p. 80); particularly deferred consequences.

Deferred consequences

Some behaviour consequences will need to be *immediate*: taking dangerous
scissors away from an infant being provocatively silly with a pair of
scissors, 'put those scissors on my desk – now' (Never simply snatch a pair
of scissors!), or directing an aggressive student to time-out.

Deferred consequences occur later in the 'discipline cycle'. A student is making it difficult for his classmate to actually get on with his work in the on-task phase of the lesson. The teacher makes her observational concerns clear: 'I've noticed you've got hardly any work done, Mark. I've offered to help – I know you can do the work. You're distracting Nazim. If you continue to keep chatting I'll have to arrange for you to work somewhere else in the room.' Mark starts whining and protesting. The teacher doesn't rise to the protestations, or argue, or try to 'reason'. She briefly reasserts: 'Think about it, Mark. I'll come back and check your work later.'

As she leaves him with a task-focused reminder she also gives him' take-up time' (p. 42ff). She has *deferred* the consequence of 'working away from . . . '. She has expressed it as a 'choice' (a directed 'choice' *within* the class rules); not a threat ('if you don't do the work I'll . . . ').

He continues to talk, chatter, task-avoid. She goes back several minutes later and directs him to 'bring (his) books and work over here'. She moves off as if he'll come. Most students do, albeit reluctantly, sulkily. In this our manner needs to be decisive and quietly assertive, *not* hostile or intentionally embarrassing.

Some students will refuse to go: 'No! I'm not going – move Nazim he was talking, too!' It is now pointless trying to force him 'to move' – he's got a wider audience. It is apposite to give another *deferred* consequence: 'If you choose not to move and carry on with your work, I'll need to speak to you after class.' 'I don't care!'

Sometimes students will say they 'don't care' when we indicate a consequence is (or may be) forthcoming. They say 'I don't care!' often in dismissive, sulky, even hostile, tones. When students say they don't care it can help to briefly affirm that as a teacher 'you do' care: 'I care when/if/because' – (keep the reason *brief*) and leave it at that. The key to any *deferred* consequence resides not with the teacher's 'threats' but the *certainty* of carrying out the appropriate, or necessary, consequences (p. 80).

Staying back after class

Some students will run off at the end of a lesson refusing to respond to our 'I want to see you for a few minutes at the end of the lesson'. As soon as the bell goes the student 'does a runner' (more commonly in secondary school) saying, in effect, 'You can't catch me – you're just a supply teacher you can't do anything!'

Avoid the temptation to chase the student. It looks ridiculous (especially if we're carrying a bit of weight). It's also not good for your health and adds to the entertainment of the student's peer audience. (And, if you did catch him what would you actually do?)

It's not the end of the world if a student doesn't stay back as you directed; it's only mildly irritating at most. The question is, should we take it further? It can help (in my view) to follow up the issue if you've got a free period (secondary school). I have done this many, many, times. It's time-consuming and we'll probably not 'feel like it'. However, if we make some effort we at least make clear to the student that you (as a teacher) do carry fair behaviour management through. It is important, though, not to convey an attitude of 'I've got you now! Thought you could run off? Well I've chased you to ground, you recalcitrant so and so!'

What we need to convey to the student (and the 'tribal tom-toms' of his peers) is the reasonable *certainty* of a consequential chain of events.

It will help to check with the year adviser if such a follow-up is advisable, and feasible. I normally find it helpful to either 'track' the student in another class (when I'm free) or get a message to them (via the year adviser) that 'Mr Rogers wants to see X in the year head's office at _____, for five minutes'. When 'tracking' a student in another colleague's class (during class time), it will be important to check if it is appropriate to knock on their classroom door (in the on-task phase of the lesson) and ask to speak to the student concerned for 5–10 minutes (obviously, physically away from the classroom door).

Is it worth 'the hassle'? It can be. It demonstrates that this 'follow-up' is what 'good' teachers 'normally' do. If we do not take this kind of follow-up option we at least need to let the appropriate senior colleague know.

When filling in the *appropriate* due-process paperwork, avoid the temptation to 'rubbish' the student or the school ('This idiot student said . . . or did . . . how dare they!' 'How can this school allow a reprobate like this to exist?') Keep it professional: focus on the student's *behaviour* and its effect on whatever rights were affected at the time.

Detentions

It will be important to know the detention policy of the school; for example, some schools allow professional discretion in class-teacher 'detentions' (even if that term is not used). Such 'detentions' may simply be a form of follow-up for 10–15 minutes at lunch time to clarify concerns, with a student, about their behaviour.

It will be important to know the policy:

- What sorts of behaviours reasonably occasion a teacher-based detention in one's role as supply teacher? Do we need to exercise a *referred* detention? (where we use the right 'incident report slips' – that's important(!) – and someone else in the grade team follows through with the detention at a later stage)?
- Who is the referral colleague?
- Is there a particular terminology used for detentions 'in-house' – at that school? It is important that whenever a supply teacher believes a detention is an appropriate consequence that they follow the 'in-house' due process. By using the 'right word' for 'detention' we show the students, again, that we are 'in the know'.

One detention to avoid is the *whole-class* detention. If there is any form of 'discipline' calculated to quickly lose the goodwill of a class it is this – punishing the whole class (e.g. by keeping them all in at lunch time) for the misdemeanours or disruptive behaviours of half a dozen or so students. I have seen teachers lose the goodwill of the many by including them in the appropriate consequences of the few.

Time-out

The concept, and practice, of 'time-out' has been mentioned several times in this text. Time-out is a serious, but at times necessary, aspect of school discipline.

'Time-out' basically refers to a range of teacher-initiated consequences that direct the student to 'take' *time away* from his/her peers to 'calm down', cool-off and hopefully think about his/her behaviour. This may be as basic as sitting away from the class group for five minutes (at infant/lower primary level), through to being directed to *leave* the classroom to go to a time-out place (another teacher's classroom, a senior teacher's office, even a withdrawal room set aside for 'time-out'). Some larger schools have 'staffed' time-out rooms – all teachers are rostered in their spare periods to supervise students sent to the time-out room.

It is normally not 'good practice' to direct a student to sit, or stand, outside a classroom for 'time-out'. In such cases the student is often as much (or more) of an attentional nuisance as he/she was *before* we sent him/her out of the classroom. He/she may even walk across the corridor and start distracting another class.

Some essential questions we need to consider regarding 'time-out':

1 *What sort of behaviours normally occasion a time-out consequence?* e.g. *repeatedly* disruptive behaviour where the student ignores corrective reminders; hostile, dangerous or aggressive behaviours; abusive behaviours.
2 *If we need to exercise time-out what are the options?* e.g. how do colleagues in the infant department use cool-off time in the classroom? Do they have a special name/place/or particular amount of time for students in time-out? (Hopefully there are no 'naughty seats' or 'naughty corners' or pathetic 'sin-bins')
3 *If we need to exit a child from the room for time-out how do we do it?* (Are there particular forms of words preferred?) Where do they go? (Teacher next door? Senior teacher? Deputy head?) Does the student go on their own or with another student (e.g. at infant/primary level).
4 *What do we do if a student refuses to go/leave?* Many schools have a back-up plan in such situations, a simple cue card (with the classroom number on it) that can be sent to a senior teacher with a trusted student. The senior teacher on receipt of the cue card (it says 'help' – just joking!) then comes to the room and exits the student to time-out. On rare occasions if a hostile power-seeking student refuses to leave (even for/with a senior teacher) the senior teacher will often 'calmly' direct the class teacher to exit the whole class while the senior teacher stays with the disruptive student. (If we can't get the disruptive student away from his/her audience, we can get the audience away from the student.) This is not the most elegant solution but it is significantly more effective than yelling, threatening and trying to drag the student out. Hopefully, the school will have a published policy about time-out usage included in the *supply teacher's support pack* (pp. 102–3, 118–21).

Time-out rooms/withdrawal rooms

Secondary schools often have a 'time-out room', a nominated room, set aside, where teachers can direct a student to go when they are *repeatedly* disruptive or behaving in an unsafe/dangerous/hostile/aggressive way.

It is crucial to know where that room is and whether to direct the student to take their bag (etc.) with them (normally students do not return from time-out during that lesson unless, perhaps, it is a double period).

One of the harder things to remember when directing a student from the classroom for 'time-out' is to remain 'calm' – decisive and focused on directing the students, but 'calm'. I have taught next door to colleagues who (no doubt at the end of their tether) yell and even scream at the student to 'Get out! Go on, get out! Get out of my classroom. I'm sick and tired of your pathetic behaviour!' The student goes, but with a dramatic postural flourish, adding 'Yeah well it's not *your* classroom anyway; you're not our teacher!' The student moves smartly off, out of class, in an 'I-don't-give-a-damn' stance. The teacher (foolishly) rushes after him/her wanting to get a 'last word' – maybe even wanting 'to win', 'And you'll be on detention today – I tell you that!' 'I don't care!' the student says walking off without turning around.

This is not a manufactured case example; I've heard this kind of 'exchange' a number of times over the years, from teachers who have got so frustratingly fed-up with a recalcitrant student that the teacher *just* reacts, not controlling what they say but wanting to be in a situation of perceived control. Of course the rest of the class often sees, and perceives, the very opposite. They see a student able to 'wind a teacher up', able to 'score', able to 'win'. The teacher's raised – even yelling – voice often becoming a source of 'entertainment'.

Using the regular teacher's terminology can help when exercising the time-out option as a supply teacher. Even the 'phrasing' used when a teacher directs a student to time-out can indicate that this 'new' teacher is 'clued-in'. It also gives the supply teacher a sense of professional security that they are following school-wide preferred practice.

Rude, challenging and confronting behaviour

The restless Year 9 class filed into the classroom. I had taken some care to rearrange the classroom seating into rows to hopefully be a factor in minimizing the noisy chatter.

Three female students, noticing the change in seating arrangements, went to the back of the room and started, quickly, to rearrange the seating pushing the last row of tables to the far corner of the room.

Rather than formally (and normally) begin the lesson at the front of the room I walked to the back of the room and faced the 'triumvirate'. I spoke to the girl I suspected of being the 'ringleader'. I had forgotten the girl's name . . . and asked 'What's your name, please?'

'What?!' Her questioning tone had a barely covered insouciance. 'What's your name, please?' (My tone was not confronting; it was civil, expectant of an answer.)

She leaned back, raised her eyes to the ceiling, and in a 'pouty' voice said, 'What d'you need to know my name for?' We might well feel like a swift rebuttal here ('Well you annoying so and so . . . I am your teacher for today and when I ask your name you bleedin' well give it – you got a problem with that!'). In a situation like this it is enough to firmly, *briefly*, assert our right to basic respect and *reframe* the situation.

'I'm not speaking to you rudely,' (my eye-contact was firm, stable – at least secure and confident in myself – after all she is a teenager; she is no threat to me; this is incipient, possibly habituated, challenging behaviour). I added, 'I don't expect you to speak rudely to me.'

'Gees! What rudely?'

'I'm not using a nasty tone of voice to you, I don't expect you to use a nasty, rude, tone in return.' I repeated the request for her name: 'I need to know your name; I'm the teacher taking our class today.'

Here she sighed, raised her eyes to the ceiling, looked at her classmates for some support (the class was quiet now). I had *tactically* ignored her posture (leaning back in her seat), the sighs, her little 'roll' of the head and raised eyes.

'Yeah,' (her tone was more moderately 'civil' – just), 'well my name's Tansy.'

I asked the other girls their names and briefly disciplined the trio: 'Tansy, Hayley and Sophie (. . .) you've rearranged the furniture; I set the rows up back there (I pointed behind me to the row they had broken off from). I expect the chairs/desks to go back there. Thanks.'

As I turned to walk off to the front of the class Tansy had another 'two bobs' worth'. 'We're just moving here so we can sit together, that's all!'

'I'm sure you want to sit together.' (a bit of 'partial agreement' can help – p. 50ff). 'The rows start back there. I'm ready to start the class.' As I walked off to the front of the classroom (giving them some take-up time) I could hear Tansy muttering as she put the furniture back. I ignored that and started the lesson. As the lesson progressed Tansy became a little more relationally co-operative. I also had a brief chat with her after class away from her classmates where I readdressed her 'rudeness'. The next lesson I worked with that class Tansy said, 'You with us again?' Her tone, here, was not nasty, 'just checking'. I encouraged her in her work, was normally positive and supportive during the lesson and made no reference to the previous incident. Our first meeting was a typical 'defining moment' in the teacher–student relationship. Such moments work for or against our leadership and any longer-term *workable* relationship with such students.

Sometimes we will come across students like Tansy who are 'rude', challenging, or confrontational. I'm sure that some teenagers may well have *habituated* patterns of uncaringly selfish and 'rude' behaviour (nothing new under the sun!). Such behaviour can occur at any age, though infants are not always *consciously* aware that they are 'rude' in the way they speak or act.

Our skill, as teacher-leaders, lies in our ability to assert our rights, expectations and needs to such students without trampling on their rights, needs and feelings.

Swearing

Some 'swearing' occurs as a normative outcome of frustration: 'Oh, sh*t! I thought I could get that shot.' (this from a student missing a basketball shot in the gym). Even some teachers swear when frustrated (really?). Some 'frustration' swearing may also be used to provoke a reaction in the teacher. In situations of conflict between teacher and student outbursts such as, 'What did I f___ing do? – Nothing, did I?!' are not uncommon with some students whose aim is to exercise some attentional power. In such cases an extreme reactive 'response' – 'Who the hell do you think you are speaking to? How dare you speak to me like that?' is likely to be the very 'response' the student is aiming for. While *never* ignoring such language, a 'calm', decisive response that addresses the behaviour without showing we are 'hurt' (or terribly shocked by all this) is likely to be a more effective expression of our leadership. 'That language is unnecessary and unacceptable in our classroom.' or 'We've all got a right to respect here, it doesn't include that kind of language.' When using basic, calm, assertive language it is important not to sound supercilious, patronizing or 'preaching'.

Some swearing is conversational: 'Did you see that great f___ing game the other day with Man.U? F___ing great!' I've heard students punctuate normal classroom chatting with such language. It is common in films, and some television these days, to employ 'f___ing and blinding' as part of social discourse (no doubt our students have ample adult models).

Some swearing *borders* on abuse such as when a student mutters 'a___hole', 'w_ker', 'd___head', 'f___ing bitch' 'quietly' under their breath as they walk away from the teacher. This form of swearing is not uncommon with highly challenging students. It is to be distinguished from direct swearing *at* a teacher; where the student faces the teacher and . . . On these occasions it is essential to decisively assert one's right to respect and to call the student to account. It may well be appropriate to direct a student, in such an instance, to a formal 'time-out' setting (p. 89) as a message to the other students of the total unacceptability of such language. In other words, we treat this kind of swearing as a form of intentional abuse.

Managing our frustration/anger

All teachers, at times, get angry with their students, or at least very annoyed or frustrated. Their laziness, indifference and lack of consideration, their abrupt manner, incivility and rudeness, their hostility and arrogance will, *naturally*, and justifiably (at times) occasion our anger. When we get very frustrated, or angry, it can seem (at times) to take over; the 'gap' between the emotional arousal, the event or issue we get angry about and our angry *behaviour* can seem very narrow!

Being professional in our management and discipline means being aware of our characteristic behaviour and learning how to manage ourselves in *relation* to others. This isn't easy. We know full well that repressing our angry *feelings*, 'holding it in', is not only counter-productive but unhealthy (psychologically and physically). We further know that merely venting our anger may see us doing, and saying, really unhelpful – even very damaging – things to our students.

Anger-arousal, in response to frustration about others' behaviour, doesn't tell us what to do with the 'arousal' we feel. Our *characteristic* behaviour (at least as teachers) *when* we're angry is *learned*; it is not merely triggered by anger-arousing situations. We may not be able to trace how we *learned* to 'be angry' but we did, over time, develop ways of dealing with the emotion of frustration and have similarly developed patterns of responsive language and behaviour that may, or may not, be constructive in addressing anger-provoking situations.

- It can help to be aware of the situations and circumstances that lower our tolerance to frustration. The feeling of frustration is a common indicator of the emergence of anger. The typical 'secondary behaviours' that students exhibit (the sighing, raised eyes, the whining and whingeing in response to our discipline) is a common source of frustration for most teachers. How we deal with such behaviour, in the 'emotional moment', is dependent on our consciousness about what is happening, our sense of getting very upset and how one can effectively respond (the skills of behaviour management). This is where a 'discipline plan' is an essential feature of our management repertoire.
- It can help to have an 'emotional vocabulary' when communicating unpleasant (but natural) feelings like frustration and anger. There are occasions when the word anger (in relation to a child's behaviour) is inappropriate. For example, 'I am angry that you haven't finished your work!' 'Concern', 'irritation' maybe, but not *anger* surely? When we use the word anger, or angry, we need to have some moral weight associated with what we are addressing in the student's behaviour. When a student uses a loud racist slur or sexist slur to a student (or to you, the teacher) for example, use the assertion 'I am angry about (or because) . . . ' or 'When anyone in our class uses racist language I get angry because . . . ' or 'I am disgusted when I hear *that* kind of language in our classroom. I don't expect *anyone* to use that language here.' We don't always need to use the actual words 'anger' or 'angry' to demonstrate how we feel about an issue or behaviour. 'Disgusted', 'appalled', 'furious', even 'hurt',

can (at times) all convey the intensity of emotion and feeling of injustice relative to one's anger and the incident/behaviour.

- When communicating our significant annoyance, frustration or anger it will help to keep what we say as brief as possible and focus on the behaviour without attacking the student, i.e. *'that* language', 'When you say things like *that* I get angry because . . . '. It is easy to allow emotion to carry us away into saying too much, and go well beyond asserting, to vilifying ('who the hell do you think you are, you idiot?') The skills of assertion are essential to effective management – they can be learned (See Chapter 3).

- It will never help to start arguing or quarrelling, 'fighting' with words at the point of high arousal. Far better to *de-escalate* the arousal, the tension, of the immediate emotional moment having assertively communicated how we feel and (*briefly*) why it will be important to lower the voice and make clear that 'it' (their behaviour) needs to stop, now. It is also important to firmly (but calmly) direct the audience of students back to work: 'Alright everyone, the show is over. Let's get back to work.' Often such 'de-escalation' will necessitate some formal time-out for the student to whom we have communicated our anger (p. 89).

- It will be crucial, later that day, to take time to initiate some repairing and rebuilding with the student (even if they are in the wrong). After the teacher (and student) have calmed down and (perhaps) had some time-out, it will demonstrate our professional goodwill if we approach the student to speak with and assure them we hold no grudges (hopefully) and that, 'we need to talk about what happened earlier today'. It will also be important to work through any 'secondary' consequences occasioned by the student's behaviour relative to the anger episode.

There is sound psychology and humanity in the apostle Paul's words in the New Testament, 'Don't let the sun go down on your anger'. (Ephesians 4). That 'advice' is just as relevant for supply teachers as it is for anyone.

How we explain stressful events

Seligman (1991) points out that we all have a *characteristic* explanatory style that we use when interpreting, processing and managing stressful events. If our 'explanatory style' is loaded with demands such as 'Children *should never* swear!', 'Children *must* do what I say without answering back', 'Children *should not* be rude' – when, in reality, children *do* swear, *do* answer back, *are* rude then we may find ourselves much more stressed than we need to be.

Reality, of course, has no obligation to simply (*ipso facto*) conform, or comply, to our *demands*. When some teachers say 'children *must* respect me', it often means that a student's insouciant voice tone and demeanour (sighs, 'pouts', 'clicking of tongue', 'raised eyes to the ceiling', etc.) all indicate significant lack of respect and *must* be challenged *immediately*. Consistent with the belief that 'children *must* respect their teachers' and 'good teachers *must* be in control at *all* times' such teachers will easily get drawn into the students' 'secondary behaviours' (the demeanour, the body language, the avoidance dialogue, etc.) and the 'primary' behaviours can easily get sidelined. In the case example of the teacher and the student without a pen the primary issue – p. 47ff (a student not working – intentionally or otherwise) is quickly overtaken by the teacher's over-focusing on the student's 'attitude' (the 'secondary' behaviours – Rogers, 2000a).

Of course such student behaviours as those recounted in this text are irritating, annoying, even a bit pathetic at times, but they are 'the reality' we have to address as teachers. A more realistic explanatory style would be: 'Well I *don't like* his attitude, but what can I now do, as teacher-leader, to manage this little contretemps in the least stressful way without getting drawn into this student's 'secondary' behaviours.' No we won't be saying all that in our heads in the immediate emotional moment; we will, however, not be reindoctrinating ourselves with 'musts', and 'shoulds' (e.g. 'children *must* not be rude' when, of course, they annoyingly are – the reality).

Yes, it is desirable that students show respect and co-operation to their teacher but when they don't an explanatory style that is *characteristically* demanding (rather than preferential and 'realistic') will work against our aims.

A discipline plan (p. 53ff) can be a positive and useful framework within which to address student behaviour in a more positive, less reactive, way. The last thing we think about in the immediate emotional moment is *what* to say. If we leave such a crucial aspect of our management to the mere moment (as it were) we'll find ourselves more easily drawn into self-defeating patterns of management.

Our *characteristic* self-talk is a *pattern of behaviour* that works generally for good or ill. I am not talking here about positive thinking; I am talking about what we *normally* construct as reasonable reality in our thinking, not what we may say occasionally that is negative. If we can catch ourselves 'posting psychological junk mail' (Rogers, 2000a) to ourselves we can challenge, and dispute it, reframe it and learn to address our stressful reality in more realistic, less self-defeating ways.

This is crucial on our 'bad days' when we feel we've failed in our professional role. 'I *shouldn't* have shouted, got angry', 'I *should* be a better teacher', 'I *can't stand it* when kids are rude and when I hear them swear . . . children *shouldn't* swear(!)'. (They do!)

By disputing such explanations and self-talk, and reframing or relabelling our failure we won't *feel so stressed*. This does not mean we deny what we did as a teacher may have been ineffective, unhelpful, stupid, even wrong; it does mean we don't *keep on blaming*, and *demanding* like some cognitive cybernetic loop. 'Yes we *should* have got to class earlier', 'Yes I *could* have countered that student's behaviour without being sarcastic. So *what can I do now*?', 'Yes I did get *too* angry when . . . however . . . '. Disputing and reframing means acknowledging what we did and *then* doing what we can to repair, rebuild, move on.

I have worked with some teachers who entrench their sense and feelings of failure by a stable, almost 'enduring' negative explanatory style. 'It's *all* my fault', 'It will last *for ever*' (i.e. 'what I did/said will have unrelieved ramifications), 'It will affect *everything* I do'. Failure is stressful, even painful, at times but the hurt can go away. We can learn to learn from – and even because – of our failure. (Isn't that what we teach our children?)

Learn to catch yourself speaking to yourself, learn to reframe: 'I *never* get it right', 'I *always* screw up' is reframed quickly to 'Yes I *do* fail – sometimes – what can I learn from it, how can I learn what I need to in order to do better, to cope better?' ('Not go back to that lunatic school!')

Learn that not '*everybody in our classes*' is a pain (even if quite a few are!) '*Some* students *are* difficult, *most* students did make an effort' is a more realistic, less stressful, explanation of this reality.

Our *characteristic* self-talk and our explanation of stressful events are crucial features of our behaviour. They have a direct impact on how we feel and how effectively we cope and manage our day-to-day teaching experience.

Developing colleague support in your school: supporting supply teachers – the role of the host school

. . . to carve out dials . . . thereby to see the minutes how they run, how many makes the hour full complete, how many hours bring about the day, how many days will finish up the year . . . so many hours must I tend my flock, so many hours must I take my rest, so many hours must I contemplate . . .

(Shakespeare, *Henry V, I: ii*)

One of the most common concerns that supply teacher's note is that other teachers do not always take the supply teacher seriously – 'second-class teachers', 'baby-sitters', merely 'cover teachers' are some of the epithets I've heard.

This may not be a stated view but it may well be communicated by default in such a way that even students (and parents) pick up the 'low status' perception that some teachers have of their 'supply colleagues'.

Supply teachers note that the tenor of support (colleague support) is felt, as well as experienced, even on arrival at a school (p. 8). Supply teaching can (at times) in some schools, be a 'lonely' profession. *Often*, for most of the teaching day the supply teacher is, effectively, 'cut-off' from their collegial peers. While that is, in part, true for all teachers at least those who teach regularly in the school know where, and how, the 'networks of support' work. I have been in some schools (as a visiting consultant) and seen a teacher sitting alone in the staff room looking a 'little lost' – no one seeming to make a conscious effort to engage with them. While we can argue that a teacher (in such a situation) should self-initiate social and professional dialogue surely we, as regular staff, can make it a little easier for them?

A basic first welcome

Fundamental perspective-taking should alert all regular staff in a school, including the school secretary, that one can feel a little anxious, 'disoriented', on one's 'first day of work' as it were. Being aware of how a supply colleague may feel is a fundamental precursor to colleague support.

The school secretary or administration officer, ('titles' vary) will often be the first 'official' colleague that a supply teacher will meet in a school. I say 'colleague' because that is the 'role' they will take on in terms of a basic, warm, welcome and orientation to the school. The 'supply teacher kit' (sounds like the army!) is often passed on by the 'secretary', who normally introduces their colleague to a staff member who can orient them to the staff room, to meet their 'teaching buddy' for the day (p. 102). Contrast this fundamental professional and moral support with the experiences recounted to me (and observed first-hand in some schools) of the cursory, distracted, even dismissive, 'welcome' received in some schools (p. 3).

In some schools supply teachers are not consciously welcomed, shown around, introduced to 'a buddy' for the day or even given a map of the school. Is it any wonder, in such schools, that staff feel like a mere appendage rather than a professional colleague?

As one supply teacher colleague recounted to me: 'It sounds like a minor thing, but I feel really uncomfortable going into staffrooms where people are huddled around in groups and I don't know anyone's name. It speaks volumes about the 'atmosphere' of the school, and it's just as obvious to parents (and prospective parents).' (Kristian)

What seems familiar, even easy, to the regular teacher can appear daunting to the 'temporary' colleague. When you live and work for a third of your day in a school you learn, and get used to, the idiosyncratic culture of the place. You 'know' what is not written down; those 'things', those 'ways of doing things here' – the culture of this school. Basic, human, perspective-taking should at least concede that one can feel a little strange in a new school: physical placement, movement around the place and finding one's way (particularly getting to the right class on time!); reading a new timetable; remembering key names of senior staff; knowing recess times; basic routines ('do I let the students go to the toilet during class time?'; 'do I line them up?'), 'what will I do if a student becomes repeatedly belligerent?'

Senior administration can increase a supply teacher's colleague support in a number of ways – moral support, structural support and professional support. Moral support refers to the assurance one feels that others are looking out for them: reassurance; encouragement; a word of apt commendation; offers of help ... Of course one cannot make another colleague receive support or, conversely, *feel* supported. We can, however, generate a reasonable level of 'colleague watchfulness' (Rogers, 2002) where we 'keep an eye out' for signals of concern, insecurity, confusion or stress in our colleague and offer (or at times) provide necessary and appropriate support. Sometimes this support is 'structural' – the school's policies and due process can provide a structure within which professional support even moral support can be normally enjoyed. Many, many, teachers have said how much they appreciated the moral support gained when a colleague has *tactfully* offered support when a whole class is verging on loss of control (p. 104); or when time-out options have given immediate back-up when a student is effectively holding a class to ransom (p. 105ff).

Developing a supply teacher plan: the 'kit'

Many schools provide the supply teacher with a 'kit' – a reference guide, or plan, to 'support supply teachers in our school' (while with us) (see later, p. 103). Obviously, a welcome (mundane, twee, as it sounds) and an introduction to a colleague who is available as a 'reference colleague' for the day can be very helpful. This is very important in large secondary schools. Just finding one's way around a large secondary school can create some natural anxiety, especially when one is in a hurry to find the right classroom (hence the necessity to get to class early). This support colleague, sometimes called a 'teaching buddy' (or 'teaching neighbour' in one primary school I worked in ...), is available to answer the seemingly mundane questions before the teaching day and is available in the break sessions (as need be).

'In our school we actually physically walk them through the school at the beginning of the day ... answering questions, giving advice whenever we can' (Deputy Head of primary school).

A good, readable, clear map is fundamental with key locations marked as reference points (administration, staff room, key classrooms, etc.).

The supply teacher 'kit'

The 'kit' would contain:

- a photocopy number for the day (and amount!);
- *bell times*;
- a workable, user-friendly map of the school and a *timetable* (with explanatory notes on codes – mandatory when trying to read some secondary school timetables!);
- any particular rules/routines that are applicable school-wide. At primary level each class may have a set of class rules and even a *student-behaviour agreement* that sets out such rules, the relevant rights and responsibilities, the general consequences of rule-breaking and 'time-out' considerations. It is important that supply teachers be given a copy of such *agreements* (or plans) to refer to as needed that day/week/term.

The *core routines* noted earlier (pp. 56ff) can be used to develop a simple frame of reference or checklist for grades/year groups that the supply teacher will be taking on any given day. It is important to not merely 'hand over a folder' (fait accompli – 'I've supported you with a folder. I've done 'my duty'). It will help to talk the supply colleague through the important issues such as classroom entry/seating plans/ students with special needs/toilet procedures/any particular discipline practices (e.g. time-out procedures) (see also pp. 118–21).

Introduction to the class

Many supply colleagues have made the point that while they appreciate an introduction to the class they have responsibility for, what they don't appreciate is being introduced as 'the supply' or 'relief' teacher in a tone that suggests that the supply teacher is a substitute, even a 'poor second', to their normal ('real') teacher. This is further exacerbated when the senior teacher then says to the class group, 'and if any of you muck up for Ms Snaggs you know what will happen, don't you – eh?' Here the ever so helpful deputy head turns and smiles to Ms Snaggs, who thinks that a good deal of her professional leadership (and responsibility) has just been compromised.

An out-of-control class

From time to time we will 'get landed' with a very difficult class, perhaps even a seemingly 'uncontrollable' class. As a supply teacher with such a class, the odds are well and truly 'stacked'. Some students believe they have nothing to lose. I have, occasionally, had to go into classes (as a senior teacher) that are mayhem – students running around the room, loudly yelling across the room, completely ignoring the teacher; the lateral tyranny of the peer group. Such disparate attentional and disruptive behaviour en masse is more common at secondary level than at primary level, though even in some infant classes I have had to 'escort out' key ring-leaders and quietly, professionally, offer support to the colleague at hand (see pp. 106ff).

No teacher, let alone a supply teacher, should have to cope with disparate mayhem; with two, three or more, students effectively holding the class to ransom.

Even the most confident, effective, teachers have (from time to time) had very hard-to-manage classes. We all know that invidious feeling of losing control of a group of students: six, eight, ten all being disruptive in one way or another – calling out; butting in; smart-alec comments; throwing pens; or getting out of seats – all while the teacher is trying (vainly) to engage and sustain some whole-class teaching and learning.

The first time it happens – the first time a teacher sees that things are well beyond any sense, or hope, of control, of being able to 'rein things in' – they should *immediately* send for help. That help should be given without blame, and debriefing and follow-up should occur at a later stage in the day.

'Losing' a class

When a teacher feels they are 'losing a class' the spiral of failure, defeat and disillusionment can be hard to break. A teacher needs to feel that there is colleague support available, that they are not 'rejected' as inadequate or incompetent. If the senior teacher just barges in and starts shouting at the class – to 'quieten them down' – the supply teacher often feels they, too, are being 'told-off', 'talked-down to' in front of the students. They feel their authority and leadership are being compromised.

Loss of control: asking for support

One of the concerns some of the supply teachers have is that in asking for (or requesting) support other (regular) teachers may see them as 'ineffective' or 'weak', 'unable to cope' (which may well be true), or, worse, incompetent. None of us as professionals want to be seen as incompetent, but at the same time it is unreasonable to pose totally unrealistic demands on ourselves, for example, when we are being verbally abused by several students in a classroom setting; when 'half the class' are effectively holding the class to ransom in terms of workable teaching and learning. On such occasions it is more than necessary to ask for support. It is right; it is professional.

Hopefully, most of you will work in collegially supportive schools most of the time.

As the head of department is walking up the long corridor she hears a loud, multitudinous, cacophony coming from room 15. She can hear the raucous voices – even shouting – the high-pitched laughter and the loud scraping of furniture. As she arrives outside the classroom she looks in and can quickly see her colleague's pained, stressed, face as he seeks to gain some sense of control. What should the senior teacher do at this point?

I have been in that position as a senior teacher quite a few times over the years. It behoves us, as senior teachers, not to simply assume 'the problem' or *cause* is an ineffective or (worse) an incompetent teacher. All of us can recall extremely hard-to-manage classes in our teaching career – I know I can. Classes where a few students, with collusive peer acceptance, acquiescence, or active support make the teacher's life virtually intolerable, and teaching and learning impossible.

On some occasions where such behaviour is ongoing, unchecked and not confronted it can degenerate into psychological harassment (Rogers, 2000a). Such classes can quickly sap a teacher's professional esteem, goodwill and confidence. I have met some supply teachers who have almost given up teaching because of such classes and the corresponding judgement they felt they received from some senior staff when it was suggested they were in some way 'at fault'.

In *some* schools the senior teacher does nothing supportive, perhaps a 'failing-teacher glare' through the window and a complaint to the deputy later. In other schools the senior teacher will simply march into the out-of-control class, start shouting at the students (who will often 'settle' – they know the 'game'). The senior teacher will then berate the class for five minutes and walk out (maybe taking one or two of the students out with him as an *ex parte* motion). As the senior staff member leaves their body language effectively says, *'That's* how you deal with them'. The class, too, has picked up the message about relative 'power', 'status' and 'control'.

In more collegially supportive schools where there are very challenging students and class groups, the notion of 'colleague watchfulness' is built into the fabric of the school's organizational day.

- Have a *normative* (no-blame) time-out policy and practice. The practical processes of such a policy should be made clear to the supply teacher at the outset of the day, e.g.:
  - the sorts of typical behaviours that that occasion/necessitate time-out;
  - how the teacher exercises time-out in the classroom (at infant level);
  - suggestions as to what to say when 'exiting' a student for time-out (some schools are thoughtfully careful about the choice of words and are averse to any shouting, yelling or threatening behaviours by teachers);
  - where to *send* a student (a particular class/person, place);
  - what to do if a student refuses to co-operate and effectively continues to 'hold the class to ransom';
  - Have a 'teaching buddy/partner' allocated for all supply teachers on any given day;
  - Let the supply teacher know that the school also exercises professional discretion that allows a 'passing' colleague to offer immediate support by either 'taking' one or two students out of the difficult class to another classroom or even 'cueing' the supply teacher 'to leave' the classroom (and take some personal cool-off time to regroup). In the first instance the support colleague knocks on the door. It is basic courtesy to knock (we don't barge in). The visiting, supporting, colleague then asks if they can borrow a few students, please: 'Ms Brown (. . .) do you mind if I borrow a few students for a little while?' The ringleaders, or attentional-power brokers, are very quickly

targeted and directed to leave: 'Damien, Mohamed, Troy, (it's often boys) come with me now.' The support colleague doesn't shout; they are confidently firm as they move off, away from the door, conveying an 'expectation of compliance'. I have had students say (on receipt of a call 'out' and 'away'), 'Have you got a special job for us?' ('Yes, real special,' I mutter.) We normally then escort the students in question to another classroom for 'time-out', or to the staffed time-out room (p. 91). The supply teacher can then reclaim some positive sense of class 'control'. Later that day the senior teacher will debrief with the supply teacher and if the supply teacher has an ongoing contract will put aside some time with the students to set up some accountability mediation (p. 114ff). Even the teacher next door to the troublesome class can leave their class 'unattended' (with line-of-sight) to 'pop' across the corridor (or next door) and 'invite' one or two students into their class as a form of 'time-out'.

If the class is in 'chaos' it is professionally appropriate to cue the supply teacher to leave. The universal cue my colleagues and I use is to knock and say something like, 'Mrs Smith, there's a message at the office.' This gives the supply teacher the dignified opportunity to leave the class (for the rest of that class period). The senior colleague then supervises that class until the end of that class period or (worst case scenario) until the end of the day. It is essential, later that day, to debrief with the 'supply colleague' to reassure they are OK and offer further support as is necessary.

The 'hard' class

The term 'hard' class hardly needs inverted commas! I'm sure that all supply teachers, at some stage, have come across a class that has been very difficult to manage. Some colleagues have told me they have had unbelievably 'impossible' classes where over half the class seems intent on destroying any possibility of teaching and learning. Such classes tend to be at upper primary/secondary level and often have a 'reputation' as 'hard to manage' even with their 'normal' teachers.

I had a class (as a mentor teacher) where the students started to demonstrate their reputation quickly in the corridor with comments like: 'What you doing here!' 'You gonna be our new teacher?' 'What do we need two

teachers for?' (I was there to mentor a colleague and help this class back to normalcy regarding teaching, learning.)

Case example

From the outset it seemed these Year 8 students were more interested in loud socializing, treating the classroom as an extension of 'social time' – loud calling out across the room 'Ay, Jayson, what you doing at lunchtime?' 'Melissa – you shut it alright?' (this from one girl to her friend). Students were getting out of their seat while the regular teacher was trying to speak to the whole class during instruction time; a couple of students were throwing pens across the room (one doing it purposefully so that when going to pick it up he could 'playfully' punch a classmate . . .); task avoidance; several students were calling out several times for their teacher to help them *immediately*. I spent several sessions with that class in order to reclaim a sense of shared purpose about why we, as a class group, met six times a week. I pitied any supply teacher ever having to teach the class on a one-off basis!

Classes become hard to manage for a variety of reasons: a shared group of personalities; idiosyncratic timetabling; subject area; the mix of 'reputation' and poor management; the physical area where a teacher has to teach; sometimes it is the way a class has been treated by some of their teachers: it is not uncommon for teachers A B C D to have the same class yet *rate* the class group differently.

A very common reason is for a class becoming hard to manage is the way it is (or isn't) established in the critical first meetings. (Rogers, 2000b).

Notwithstanding possible reasons why a class has become hard to manage, the supply teacher is stuck with *that* class, *that* day or *that* timetable slot – sometimes with, sometimes without, warning.

The 'effective' solutions to 'cracking a hard class' are long term – they will always necessitate re-establishing a workable and positive sense of what it means to be a learning community. They require a year-level commitment to colleague support, often with collegial mentoring; a genuine attempt and student involvement at a 'fresh start' through shared needs-analysis, and a *teacher–student behaviour agreement* regarding learning and relational behaviours within class time. A fresh start will always necessitate practical realities such as rights, responsibilities and routines – routines as basic as a workable entry to class, seating arrangements, noise levels (within class time), how to fairly (and appropriately) get teacher-assistance during on-task learning time, through to tidy-up and considerate exit from the classroom (Chapter 5).

Quite often such core routines have not been thoughtfully and persistently established in the critical first weeks of first term. 'Hard class' groups will often habituate poor, inadequate or inappropriate behaviours when their teachers do not thoughtfully and carefully establish their class from day one, week one. There is a natural readiness, in a group of students, about the establishment phase of the year with their grade/class teacher. If that 'readiness' is not developed for the habituated good of all it will be that much harder for the supply teacher to seek to re-effect positive expectations in the course of *one* lesson, or over one day.

Making a fresh start with a class

For supply teachers who have to 'cover' a class for several weeks or for a whole term the 'hard' class issue needs collegial approach from the *very first* meeting. Because the supply teacher will be with the class for several weeks it will be important to give the class the opportunity to talk out issues of common concern and then, with their new teacher, to develop a 'fresh start' for this term.

The students may not have really liked their regular teacher, or conversely they may have had a strong attachment, a sense of stable security with their 'normal' teacher, his/her place to be taken by you – the supply teacher. Either way the students may show their 'discomfort', their concerns and anxieties, their 'grief', even their animosities, by 'taking it out' on the new teacher. It is essential that the incoming supply teacher plans how to communicate his/her role and relationship with such a class. It will help to discuss with the grade/year head any special concerns or issues relevant to the grade/class and to request this discussion prior to their first meeting with the class.

After the preliminary 'good morning/welcome' on that first morning it will be important to assure the class that 'you' (their new teacher) cannot replace Ms/Mr _____ but that you will do your best to work *with* the class and that you need their co-operation and support 'so that we can enjoy our time together'. It will also be important (particularly at infant and lower primary level) to keep the 'old' secure routines and procedures in place, even seating plans (if such routines had all previously contributed to a workable cohesion). If the class were known to have had a strong, positive, relational bond with their previous teacher, the class may be going through a form of 'grieving' at the 'loss' – the 'going'. It can often help to have some 'circle-time' (classroom meeting) to give individual class members an opportunity to talk out their feelings and concerns. At such a meeting it will be important to have a senior colleague present (who knows the class) to clarify the purpose of such a meeting and to reappraise 'circle-time rules' before embarking. 'Tell me about your teacher . . . what was she like?'

Your professional task (as supply teacher) is not to emulate the previous teacher but to assure the class that:

I know you all really cared about Ms/Mr _____ . It must be hard not having Ms/Mr _____ here with you every day. You really enjoyed Ms _____'s teaching; many of you have said how much you miss her . . . I can understand that . . . I know you will help me, like you helped Ms _____..

I cannot be the same as Ms _____ , obviously, but I will try hard – with your help – to make our grade/class time the best it can be . . . while I'm with you.

It will also be important to reappraise the class behaviour plan (p. 70): 'I know Ms _____ had some rules she had developed with you' (show you are aware of the classroom rules, even republishing them again as a reference point); reappraise core routines (p. 56ff) and do not hesitate to positively discipline wherever necessary from day one. I have worked with supply teachers who will 'overlook' behaviours like calling out, butting in, talking while the teacher is talking, inappropriate class noise (during learning-task time) etc. in the mistaken view that by doing so they are 'softly-softly' building a 'relaxed' relationship. In fact they are habituating patterns of behaviour that may prove difficult to refocus in the weeks ahead.

From day one, first period, it is important *positively* to establish and affirm our leadership by addressing such behaviours (p 10ff) and, where necessary, to follow up with individuals after class time (p 79ff).

The 'circle-time' approach is not to excuse any latent ill will (or active attentional-hostility). It is to assure the class that you are aware of where they have been, how they feel and the need to go on *being* a positive class; a class group that supports learning, supports the behaviours that help us all here and support their new teacher. We then (of course) need to earn their respect and goodwill by the quality of our leadership and teaching.

Repairing and rebuilding: when the class has given the relief teacher a really hard time

From time to time a class will have made the supply teacher's life really, really unpleasant (p. 104). On these occasions it behoves the senior teacher to effect some appropriate repairing and rebuilding, even 'restitution'.

Even if the supply teacher is no longer 'present' in the school it will still be important for a senior teacher to visit that class and make clear what is was that 'many' students (not all) did on the day Ms/Mr was there with them:

- Communicate your very serious concern about their behaviour(s). It will not help to attack them, e.g. 'You pack of animals, you are a disgusting class – a shame to our school (*that* may be the truth); who the hell do you think you are?' A long, vitriolic lecture will see immediate frowning ('What us?') and, while the class evidence seemingly passive 'compliance', it will not change anything in the long term.
- It will be important to communicate how you feel (as a teacher on behalf of all teachers who teach here): 'Yesterday Ms/Mr Smith was here as your teacher for the day. A number of you made her/his time with you really, really difficult and very unpleasant. I have a note here – repeated calling out; students using loud voices during class work; students wandering and hassling other students; some students refusing to work.' (It is important that the senior teacher not label *all* the class as having engaged in 'making Mr _____/Ms _____'s day horrible'.)

    'I am *very* upset that anyone in *our* school – *our* school – would treat another human being like that. I'm not saying it was all of you but the rest of you in 9D allowed students, here, to do and say things that really made it virtually impossible for Ms/Mr to teach here yesterday. I would have expected better of you.'

    'Ms/Mr could be your mum/dad/sister . . . Ms Smith is a person – not someone you can just hassle!'

    'I have a list of things that members of class did and said here. I want you to think about what happened yesterday and I want you to work out how you can apologize to Ms/Mr Smith.'

    Often, at this point, the class is seriously quiet; they have felt your anger (not your aggression) at the total unfairness of the behaviour of many in the class group. It is important to, now, de-escalate the arousal (of feelings) and direct their energy and thinking time to what they (as a class group) can do to try to 'repair and rebuild'.
- Invite them to think about how the teacher would have felt and ask them how they will make their apologies, in writing through a

'composite' class letter. This is something I have done before with class groups. It offers a chance for a valid expression of feelings, reflection on *group* (as well as individual) behaviours and gives the opportunity for some restitutional healing.

- It is essentially about perspective-taking, and while it may not 'reach' all students it will reach most students, and that matters. It's worth it.
- Ask the class what they need to do *next time* a supply teacher comes to take their class.

'I want you, as a class, to discuss quietly (in pairs) what sorts of ways we – as a class group – can make a supply teacher's life more enjoyable *next time*. I want you to come up with suggestions as to what we can do, say, a kind of plan if you like. I'll take up your suggestions later in the lesson and give you feedback on how we can make them work for us. I'll have another meeting with you on _____ . In the mean-time I'll pass on your written apologies to Mr/Ms Smith.'

For those teachers in long-term supply cover, similar approaches can be part of repairing and rebuilding and a helpful precursor to a 'fresh start' with the class.

It is also important that the supply teacher not hold any grudges, residual hostility or 'revenge' against the class. While it is natural to feel upset, even angry, at seemingly whole-class disruption, I have found that when we write back or even revisit the class group to re-effect our goodwill, it is actually possible to rebuild a working relationship and demonstrate that humanity essential to good teaching and positive rela-tionships.

Students who harass (supply) teachers

In some classes, in some schools, there are students who calculatingly, purposefully, set out to hassle – even harass – a teacher. They will most often excuse it as 'fun' or just 'mucking around' or 'no big deal'. Such students often have a group of collusive 'hangers-on' who support such harassing of the supply teacher.

Some teachers find it difficult to assert themselves as teacher-leaders or their physical/psychological presence, as perceived by students, presents as 'weak' or 'fair game'. Such teachers sometimes let students say totally unacceptable things in their hearing, or engage in persistently attentional behaviour without the teacher firmly asserting due discipline.

The sorts of behaviours that some supply teachers face range from repeated attentional and power-confronting behaviour through to verbal abuse: 'This class is crap', 'This is all bullsh*t!', 'Don't have to do no f_____ work here!', 'Don't take any notice of her!', 'He's useless'; homophobic slurs (suggestive or spoken) even 'incipient threats'.

If you believe you have been harassed by a student(s) it is crucial that you report this at the first instance (that day) and professionally expect that you will have the opportunity to confront the student(s) in question at some stage (even if it means coming back into the school after the day's supply teaching).

The least helpful thing to do if one has been 'bullied' (psychologically harassed) is to hold it in, not say anything, or (just as bad) make 'light of it' for fear other colleagues may see you as 'weak', 'unable to cope', ineffective or (worse) incompetent. I have worked with teachers who have stressfully held in such harassment for weeks, only to finally 'collapse'. as it were, emotionally strung-out or have simply thrown in the towel rather than confront such bullying (for that is what it may well be) as early as possible.

In such circumstances it is often beneficial for the school to set up an accountability mediation (Rogers, 2000b) meeting with each of the perpetrators and the teacher who has been on the receiving end of such harassing behaviours. Such a meeting – between the perpetrators (student(s)) and victim (teacher) – needs the support of a senior staff member in discussing the issues concerned, planning for the meeting, facilitating and conducting the key phases of the meeting, and (where necessary) initiating consequences to the student(s) concerned.

The purpose of such a 'meeting' is to give the supply teacher the opportunity to confront the students (one at a time) about their harassing behaviours, and expect appropriate apologies and assurances that such behaviours will not occur again.

It is not an opportunity for some psychological revenge (tempting as that might be!) The 'tone' of the teacher confronting the student needs to be serious, focused on the behaviour of the perpetrators and not lecturing or hectoring. As 'victim' it is important not to dwell on one's feelings (this may only serve to act as grist to the bullies' distorted self-esteem mill). Emphasize, rather, the effect of the student's bullying *behaviour* on the teacher's rights. Here it will help to refer to the school's rights/responsibility code and the school's 'anti-bullying' policy.

- It is crucial that the supply teacher establishes the facts clearly with their senior teacher colleague, particularly the *typical* and frequent things the student has said, suggested or done. Focus on the student's behaviour, (even 'suggestive' – non-verbal – behaviours can be tantamount to bullying when they are repeated and intentional).
- Have these relevant facts written down beforehand – before conducting any meeting with students. The senior teacher will plan with their supply teacher colleague how to conduct the meeting, what sorts of issues to cover, how to address the student's typical 'discounting' of their behaviours ('I wasn't the only one!' 'Other students did stuff too!' 'It's no big deal.' 'I was only joking.' 'I don't care anyway!' 'Maybe they did – your responsibility is . . .' 'We will be speaking to the other students . . . we're talking about *your* behaviour now.'
- Set aside an appropriate, convenient time for the supply teacher, senior teacher and students – during a school day.
- Conduct such a meeting individually with students not (normally) as a group.
- The purpose of the meeting is made clear to the student at the outset of the meeting and he/she is reminded he/she will have the opportunity to 'have his/her say' later.
- The 'victim' (the teacher) needs to clearly, and briefly, confront the student by:
  – explaining what is was the bully did (what they said *or* suggested);
  – explaining how such behaviour affects the teacher's right to teach, their right to basic respect;
  – that such behaviour is *totally* unacceptable in our school; that it must stop, and an assurance is called from the student about what they will need to *do* to make such behaviour stop.
- The perpetrator is allowed a right of reply but is directed to apologize and give assurances such behaviours will not occur again.

It is important that supply teachers be accorded such rights (to address the perpetrators of any bullying/harassment) and to debrief with senior staff.

Students with emotional-behavioural disorders

Supply teachers will invariably be teaching in classrooms with students who present with emotionally-disordered patterns of behaviour. Sometimes these students have been diagnosed as such (EBD); they may be on medication for their behaviour disorder (such as Ritalin or dexamphetamine for attention deficit [hyperactive] disorder – ADHD).

It is important to know if such students are in your classes – not to create some negative self-fulfiling prophecy but to be as supportive as possible in your management.

- Such students are often on particular forms of 'contracts' or *individual behaviour management* plans. These 'plans' assist such students with self-management skills. It will be important – even for a day's supply teaching – to know how these plans work on a day-to-day basis and how (as supply teacher) to give feedback and monitoring to the student within their 'individual' plan.
- There may be particular 'cues' or forms of language used by the regular teacher that help in management and discipline contexts. Such 'cues' often give a sense of stability, and a sense of focus, for students with EBD and can easily be appropriated by supply teachers.
- There are often particular forms of *time-out plans* for students with EBD behaviours. Such 'plans' may even include a particular case-supervisor who can be called on in time-out situations. Schools will, normally, make such 'individual' forms of time-out clear to supply teachers at the outset of a teaching day.
- Such students *normally* may be required to sit with nominated students (for peer support) or in a nominated place in the room during on-task learning times. It will be worth checking on this likelihood of prepared (or required) seating arrangements at the outset of the day to avoid any angst later.
- In some schools with particularly challenging student behaviours the student concerned will be 'enrolled' in another classroom for the day his regular teacher is away. This minimizes unnecessary stress for the student, the supply teacher and the grade in question.

Students with severely challenging behaviours

A school administration needs to give some thought to the management of students with more demanding expressions of EBD behaviour. As mentioned above, it can often help to 'enrol' such students in another grade/class just for the day that the regular teacher is away. The very least we can do (as a senior administration team) is to have a clear, workable, time-out plan to assure the supply teacher that if a student does become very difficult to manage they can send for a senior teacher to come and 'exit' the student from the classroom for that class period time (p. 89ff).

Repairing and rebuilding

Making the effort to 'go back' to a student even during class time to make time to speak with them, to apologize where necessary, is a crucial aspect of our professionalism as a teacher. It is also an essential feature of relationship-building (even on a single teaching day).

Even if we are not 'at fault' it will be important for us to demonstrate we care enough to have a 'chat' with a student we have had to discipline, at some stage, to show there are no grudges held, no residual animosity. This is crucial if we have said things in the 'heat of the moment' which are inappropriate, unprofessional or hurtful.

Honestly focusing on what it was that was hurtful in what we said is enough; we don't need to 'plead our case' or 'beg forgiveness'. An honest 'I'm sorry I said . . .' is enough, and then move on even if, sometimes. a student does not appear to accept our apology. It is very disconcerting when a teacher displays uncivil, rude or arrogant behaviour in choosing not to exercise the basic humanity of repairing and rebuilding.

Sometimes it will be helpful to let the student (or group) know we are 'sorry that . . .' (as distinct from 'I'm sorry *for*. . .') This is important if we have had a 'bad day' with a class. Tempting as it may be it won't help to berate them *all*, 'You're the worst class I have ever taught in my entire life! You're rude, you're nasty – I don't know how your teacher puts up with you. You're nothing but a pack of . . . ! I'm glad I won't ever have to teach you again!' (One of the students whispers to a classmate – 'So are we!')

I've actually heard diatribes like that; one can only imagine how such a teacher will be perceived by the students, teachers and parents. Imagine how different the end of the session or day might be if the teacher has said something like, 'Look folks – I know we've had some ups and downs today, but we did get some work done.' I wish you well – all of you.'

Core routines for classroom organization, teaching and management

It will be worth checking how these routines operate in 'your school'. It will also be helpful for team leaders and year heads to reassess the consistency of such 'routines' as they operate across the school and how these routines can be communicated to supply colleagues (see also pp. 53–6).

- *Class roll/timetable and 'bell signal' times and length of class periods*: this is basic but crucial. We don't want to be dithering around asking students or hassling colleagues halfway through a lesson. What are the regular teacher's name(s) for that grade/class (or the periods I teach, say, at secondary level)? It will help to know the regular grade/subject teacher's name in your welcome to the class and in assuring the class you 'know what Ms Snaggs usually does' (when it comes to class routines/activities).
- Are there any particular *classroom entry procedures* (pp. 57–8)?
  - Do children line up (particularly infants; do they go in single file, pairs)?
  - How are coats/hats/bags normally processed 'before' or 'on entry'?
  - Do students go straight to their desks/table groups? Carpet time (infants)?
  - How is 'carpet time' (infants) normally organized? (Even fundamental routines like these can give some sense of security and continuity between what the regular teacher does and what the supply teacher can do.)
  - *Assembly* (form/year assembly): Is the supply teacher required to stay with their nominated class *during* assembly?
- *Seating plans*: Is there a normal seating plan for that grade/or class, or is it ad hoc, as it often is in secondary schools?
  - Are there any particular students who should not be sitting together in this class?

- *Establishing whole-class attention* at the beginning of each class period:
  - Are there particular 'cues'/'signals'/forms of 'verbal cueing' used by the regular teacher or department? This can be very important at infant level where very young children may not always understand a new teacher's idiosyncratic forms of words. I worked in an infant school (UK) where the universal whole-class cue for attention ('eyes, ears this way') was a teacher's raised hand; a non-verbal, school-wide, cue used by all staff. Even that simple aide-memoir was a help to my teaching time at that school.
  - In some classes (at infant and middle primary) there is a mutual greeting time between teacher and class, and a 'morning talk' time, that allows a 'social-breather' between home and school day. In many Catholic schools it is normal practice to begin (and end) the day with a prayer-time.
- *Classroom rules* and key school rules: are there any *published* classroom rules for behaviour and learning? Is there a published *classroom behaviour agreement* (p. 70)? It will help, as a matter of course, to take your own set of rules covering key stages/ages of students (see pp. 15, 68ff). Key school-wide rules to be aware of are things like chewing gum/eating in class/mobile phone and Walkman use (secondary). Students sometimes manage to get some supply teachers flummoxed even on issues like chewing gum and eating in class. Short-term supply teachers are not normally required to address uniform/dress-code issues (though they might refer it on).
- *Materials and resources*: It will help to know if the class group has 'monitors' for materials/resources. (It won't help to have half a dozen loud volunteers clamouring to hand out class equipment/resources.) It will help to know where there are spare textbooks (secondary) or if there are class sets. At primary level normal, daily, routines such as take-home readers will need to be continued by supply teachers. How such regular whole-class routines are carried out will normally be included in the supply teacher kit (p. 54).
- *Toilet procedures*: It is important to know if there is a set routine for leaving the room to go to the toilet: any time? How many children? At infant level children normally go in pairs, even at middle and upper primary there may be a health/safety policy allowing children to go to the toilet in pairs. At secondary level there is normally a 'toilet pass'

system that the supply teacher needs to be acquainted with.
- *Transitional routines*: those routines between instructional and 'on-task learning time' such as:
  - noise level maintenance in the room (these may be set monitoring routines/cues) (p. 71ff);
  - how to get teacher assistance;
  - marking of work: do the students 'take' the work to the teacher or place their work in a 'to-be-marked' tray'; does the teacher normally rove the room and transitionally mark?
  - does the regular teacher have normative rotating work groups (at primary)?
  - students who are 'early finishers' or who do not complete the work: is there a range of options students can choose when finished early (assuming they have checked/edited their work)? Do we need to direct students to stay back to finish significantly uncompleted work? Many secondary supply teachers find this issue of particular concern – the few students who do almost no on-task work during the lesson – is there a procedure for referring such student behaviour to the class regular teacher?
- *Students with special needs*: It is important the supply teacher know which children have been targeted for special needs in learning or behaviour (often both). The special needs teacher will give guidance in this area. Such children are often on individual education plans (IEPs) and/or individual behaviour management plans (IBMPs). Knowing how such plans work with particular children and how, as supply teacher, you can support and encourage the child within such a plan will account for a more satisfactory day all round. Children with particular medical, or 'behaviour-disorder' needs (such as ADHD) may be on special medication. Supply teachers, as a matter of course, should be notified of such children in their classes.
- *Specialist teachers* (at primary level): Does the supply teacher escort the grade 2 class to/from specialist classes (other Languages, music, art, phys. ed.)? Do they then stay with the class during specialist teacher's period?
- *End of session/end of day* routines: are there class monitors (primary) who help organize resources/computers, pot-plants?

- Letters/notices home?
- Class reminders for the following day?
- Is there 'circle-time' at the end of the day or week (at primary)? Certainly a brief summary and recap prior to a positive, 'formal', goodbye should be normative; par for the course.
- On a Friday, at primary level, some students may be allowed to take class pets home – what is the procedure to take home the class 'gorilla' (how do we cage and sign off, etc.)?

It is essential that the supply teacher make a conscious decision and concentrated effort to work with the class to leave the room tidy, particularly at the last period of the day (if the classroom is left in a 'pig-sty' one can hardly *simply* blame the students). Leaving the room tidy is something we should do as a professional *matter of course*. Even a simple issue like 'lost property' needs to be considered – do we 'sign-it-off' leave it there?

Much of this is professional common sense, of course, but it will help to enable a smoother running, more supportive day (for students and supply teacher alike).

Conclusion

Ask most teachers why they went into teaching and a common answer will include that they wanted to 'make a difference'. Most supply teachers, too, have said much the same. Like their 'full-time' colleagues they take their professional role and responsibilities seriously. Most teachers teach because they want to; they chose this profession. That, I hope, has been the underlying message of this book – we are professionals. A supply teacher is *a teacher* – 'full stop'.

We bring to the supply teacher role all the professional acuity and necessary skill of a 'regular' teacher. We enhance the profession of teaching itself when we consciously address the daily or weekly supply teaching role with the sorts of skills, attitudes, expectations and planning discussed here.

It is my hope that this book will encourage and support that kind of professionalism.

References and suggested reading

Kyriacou, C. (1991) *Essential Teaching Skills*. Basil Blackwell, London.

Robertson, J. (1997) *Effective Classroom Control: Understanding Teacher Pupil Relationships*, 3rd edition. Hodder and Stoughton, London.

Rogers, B. (1999) Research is discussed at length in: Rogers, B. (2002) *I Get By With a Little Help: Colleague support in schools*. Australian Council for Educational Research, Camberwell, Victoria.

Rogers, B. (2000a) *Classroom Behaviour: A Practical Guide to Effective Teaching, Behaviour Management and Colleague Support*, Paul Chapman Publishing, London.

Rogers, B. (2000b) *Cracking the Hard Class: Strategies for Managing the Harder than Average Class*. Paul Chapman Publishing, London.

Rogers, B. (2002) *I Get By With a Little Help: Colleague Support in Schools*. Australian Council for Educational Research, Camberwell, Victoria.

Seligman, M. (1991) *Learned Optimism*, Random House, London.

Thody, A., Gray, B. and Bowden, D. (2000) *The Teacher's Survival Guide: How Do I Deal with Difficult Behaviour? How Do I Cope with the Stress of Work? How Do I Manage my Workload and Other School Commitments and Still Have a Life?* Continuum Press, London.

NOTE
A Teacher Support Network is available to all teachers – including supply teachers – offering a wide range of support from personal to professional:

The *Teacher Support Line* (Teachers' Benevolent Fund)
Tel: 0800 562 561
www.teachersupport.info

Index